First Aid for Police Firearms and Clos Protection Officers

For Community, Custody, Firearms (D13), Tactical and Police Medics

By Chris Breen, RGN, Paramedic

Dedication

Many people have helped in this project; I would like to thank Caroline Jackson for all her support and proof-reading,

Updates

If you were like to receive information on updates, corrections and new editions. Or if you have any suggestions for new content. Please email me at;

chris.breen@aol.co.uk

D13 ENHANCED (AUTHORISED FIREARMS OFFICERS) 187

APPENDIX 1 MEDICAL TERMINOLOGY.............213

Introduction

Chris Breen is a Paramedic and an Emergency Nurse Practitioner who served with the RAMC and is currently a Clinical Tutor with additional qualifications in Trauma and Remote Medicine. He has been involved in Police first aid training from basic to enhanced D13 levels and has acted as an expert assessor for officers in training in the medical management of road traffic collisions. He is also involved in Joint Emergency Service interoperability (JESIP) Tactical and Operational Training.

The aim of this work is to provide the officers with the knowledge and skills to deal with a variety of medical conditions and traumatic injuries beyond the scope of normal first aid which they may potentially encounter during their duties.

The book covers equipment, First aid supplies and initial first aid treatment. If the injury or illness would benefit from more advanced measures then these are detailed as well as any skills needed to carry them out. The British Medical association (BMA) have published guidance on the "Health care of detainees in Police stations". A large proportion of detainees will be vulnerable for a number of reasons; this could be due to poverty, mental health issues or drug or alcohol dependence. These can lead to medical problem which can potentially affect them whilst detained. The Custody Officer is responsible for the care and treatment of detainees including the provision of food, drink, human contact, warmth, sleep, exercise, personal hygiene, clothing, protection from injury and medical treatment. Medical assessment and or treatment may need to be carried out on any detainees, those held due to immigration issues, those living on the streets, persons with mental health issues or those that are intoxicated through drink or drugs and that require a place of safety.

A custody officer may require additional support in the care of detainees from a Health Care Professional; this could be a Doctor, Nurse or Paramedic.

Fitness for detention

• assessment of illness (physical or mental)/injuries/drug and alcohol problems

• advice to custody officer on general care while in custody

• provision of necessary medication

• referral to hospital

• admission under mental health legislation

Fitness for interview

- assessment of competence to understand and answer questions
- where the patient is mentally ill or mentally vulnerable, advising on the need for an

appropriate adult

- advising on any special provisions required during interview
- reassessment after interview

Forensic examination

- assessment and recording of injuries (including injured Police officers)
- interpretation of injuries
- collecting samples, eg blood to test for toxicology and intimate samples (eg in murder or rape cases)
- Road Traffic Act 1988 and Road Traffic (Northern Ireland) Order 1995 cases

Therapeutic assessment and treatment

- for illness
- for injuries sustained
- advice to custody officers on general care while in custody
- provision of necessary medication
- provision of a report of any illness or injuries requiring attention to be passed to other health professionals when the detainee is transferred.

In the case of minor injuries or illness the custody officer can decided not to contact a medical professional if they are in any doubt then one should be called. However if the detainee requests to see someone this must be done.

In all cases good first aid skills are essential to treat and or stabilise the casualty until further assistance arrives.

Source

BMA (2009) Health care of detainees in police stations

Contents of Modules

Module 1 Basic Life Support.

Module 2 First Aid Skills Police (Emergency First Aider at Work).

Target Group.

All Police Officers and Police Staff who have direct contact with the public.

Duration 1 day. This training will be repeated every three years.

Learning Outcomes.
Manage a first aid scene.
Assess a casualty.
Perform adult basic life support (including child and infant).
Manage a choking casualty (including child and infant).
Place a casualty in the recovery position.
Report casualty information.
Manage a casualty with shock.
Manage a casualty with chest pain.
Manage a casualty who is bleeding.
Manage a casualty with spinal injury.
Manage a casualty who is convulsing.
Manage the control of infection.
Manage a casualty with a head injury.
Manage a casualty who has been poisoned.
Recognise Excited Delirium and Acute Behavioural Disorder.

Module 3 Custody First Aid.

Target Group.

All Police Officers and Police Staff who are responsible for the care of detainees.

Duration. 1 day. This training will be repeated on annual bases.

Learning Outcome.
This module will incorporate the first aid skill covered in module 1 and 2 and in addition addresses range of medical situations that personnel working in a custody environment are likely to encounter.
Measure respiration.
Manage a casualty who is having an asthma attack.
Manage a casualty who has fainted.
Manage a casualty who is convulsing.
Manage a casualty with unstable diabetes.
Manage the control of infection.
Manage the control of infestations.
Manage the use of ligature removing devices.
Demonstrate safe use of Automated External Defibrillator(AED)

Module 4.
First Aid at Work; Initial and Requalification.

Target Group.

Police Officers working in a specialist role that requires a higher level of first aid than module 1 and 2. First Aiders for Police Buildings.

Duration 3 days. Refresher training undertaken annually.

Learning Outcomes.

This module is the First Aider at Work (FAW) Standard as defined by the Health and Safety Executive (HSE).

Introduction and Legislation
Managing Infection Control
Primary survey DRSABC overview
Secondary survey, Action plans and recovery position
Taking a Medical History
Placing Casualty in the Recovery Position
Breathing problems
Manage a choking casualty
Anaphylaxis & Epi- pen
Asthma and Hyperventilation
Manage a casualty who is having an asthma attack.
Basic Life Support (BLS)
Manage a casualty with shock
Managing a patient with chest pain
Treating a casualty that is Bleeding
Internal bleeding
Chest injuries and crush syndrome
Manage a casualty with unstable diabetes.
Manage a casualty with a head injury.
Stroke
Manage a casualty who is convulsing.
Managing Burns
Skeletal Injuries
Eye injuries

Module 4/ D13 Enhanced.

First Aid at Work; Initial and Requalification.
Target Group Authorised Firearms Officers.
Duration 4 days. Refresher training undertaken annually.
Learning Outcomes.

This module is the First Aider at Work (FAW) Standard as defined by the Health and Safety Executive (HSE).

This module will be further supplemented with the addition of the D13 enhanced tactical medicine that must be delivered by trainers who have experience in pre-hospital care.

It will involve moulages to replicate the provision of trauma care whilst in a conflict situation and the trainers will be assisted by a National Firearms Instructor.

Additional training will also be required for:

Use of nasopharyngeal airways.

Use of oropharyngeal airways.
Use of oxygen therapy.
Use of suction devices.
Use of haemostatic dressings.
Identification of wound management techniques including dressing and packing for all types of wounds.

First Aid at Work;

Initial and Requalification.
Target Group. Police Officers working in a specialist role that requires a higher level of first aid than module 1 and 2. First Aiders for Police Buildings.

Duration 3 days. Refresher training undertaken annually.
Learning Outcomes. This module is the First Aider at Work (FAW) Standard as defined by the Health and Safety Executive (HSE).

Introduction and Legislation

First aid is immediate aid provided by non-medical people which aims at Preserving Life, preventing deterioration and promoting the casualties recovery, knows as the three P`s.

(P)reserve Life

- Ensure the Scene is Safety for yourself and the casualty

- Perform a Primary Survey to identify life threatening conditions

- Administering Life Saving Aid

(P)revent Deterioration

- Fully Assess for additional Injuries and illnesses.

- Perform a secondary survey.

- Perform Emergency First Aid

(P)romote Recovery

- Relieve discomfort and anxiety, keeping patient warm or cool

- By providing reassurance

- By notifying Ambulance Services or referring on

Upon successful completion of a First Aid at Work Course you will be qualified for 3 years as a First Aid at Work First Aider in accordance with the following legislation;

- Health and Safety at Work Act 1974
- Health and Safety (First Aid Regulations) 1981

Managing Infection Control

In order to manage infection control, wash your hands or use disinfectant gel or spray before that after treating a casualty.

Wear disposable gloves and sometimes disposable aprons, masks and/ or eye protection as appropriate

Place all contaminated items in a suitable container for disposal such as soiled dressings or clothing. If an ambulance is in attendance they will sometimes take clinical waste with them to dispose of at hospital or at their own base.

Primary survey, DRSABC overview

In order to diagnose an illness or ascertain the extent of an injury a history and full patient examination should be made.

History taking and examination is just practice. It isn't difficult; the trick is to know what is abnormal. When you are first learning clinical examination you should practice examining people who are not ill; partners, children, and friends, as many as you can convince to let you do it. The purpose of this is to know what is normal. Once you achieve this it becomes much easier to recognise the abnormal.

Getting started (The 60 second assessment)

Before you touch or speak to the patient take a mental step back and look at the patient - an 'end of bed' assessment.

It doesn't matter if the presenting complaint is a sprained ankle or massive trauma, you should apply the same basic concept to every patient you see.

This initial survey can tell you a lot about them.

How do they appear? Are they pale, sweaty, shaking, do they appear anxious?

How are they sitting are they holding an injured or tender part of their body?

Do they appear to be struggling to breathe?

Can you hear any wheeze or rattle when they breathe?

Shake their hand. Does it feel cold? What is their capillary refill time?

Is there anything around that gives clues to the situation?

Don`t overlook the obvious ask the patient what's wrong, they might have experienced it before and know what the problem is and what needs to be done to resolve it.

In patient assessment the aim is for early identification of any potentially life threatening problems sometimes referred to as 'Red Flag indicators'. The extent of an illness or injury can be judged on a sliding scale usually defined as being between 'Well' and 'Very sick' or 'Big sick'. It is usually easier to say if a patient is at either end of the scale but more difficult to place where a patient is along the length of the scale.

This initial information helps you identify sick vs. not sick, but also what your ongoing assessment needs to be the trauma / critical ill primary and secondary survey approach or the more slow paced and system specific medical assessment.

Trauma Assessments

The full sequence below is primarily aimed at a seriously injured trauma patient, but elements of the assessment can be applied to any patient and apply just as equally to the initial assessment of a sick medical patient. The more stable the patient is the slower and more relaxed the history and examination can be.

Patient Position

Always consider the most appropriate patient position for examination. If the patient may have suffered serious traumatic injury before examination lay the casualty flat on their back. If collapsed and unconscious but without injury consider placing them in the recovery position. If conscious sit or lay as appropriate, they should be encouraged to adopt the most comfortable position. If shock is suspected then lay them down and raise legs, unless they are injured. If shocked and breathless, support head and shoulders but still raise legs if practical.

The patient also needs to be appropriately exposed. It's important to respect the patient's modesty, but not at the expense of being able to see exactly what is going on. If you don't uncover it you cannot see it. Modesty frequently causes sub-optimal assessment, so try and strike a balance.

An approach

First Aid students are taught the DRS ABC Primary Survey approach to casualty examination this will identify life threatening problems with the casualty and its equally applicable here. DRS ABC stands for;

- Danger
- Response
- Shout for or get Help
- Airway
- Breathing
- Circulation

If the patient is conscious and talking then it is safe to assume that they have a clear airway and an adequate breathing rate and pulse. But these observations still might not be normal due to illness and injury so still need to be assessed.

If a patient has a problem with their airway this needs attention before moving on. Without a patent airway both breathing and circulation are quickly compromised. Similarly a problem with breathing needs to be resolved before circulation is assessed.

The main aims of care in these circumstances can be described as follows;

To (P)reserve the casualty's condition

To (P)revent deterioration in the casualty's condition

To (P)romote Recovery

These are collectively known as the three P's.

As discussed above, there are two basic type of examination firstly one for trauma patients who have had an accident or have been injured or are medically seriously unwell and secondly those who have a less serious medical problem. Many parts are common to the two types of assessment. When performing a medical assessment each body system needs to be assessed. Once you have a better knowledge of clinical assessment you can be more focused and just look at the systems you believe are effected (or the presenting problems), but while learning examine each system.

When providing more in depth care the DRS-ABC sequence is expanded to DRS-ABCDEFGHI, doing a full assessment of the casualty.

D- Danger:

Danger can come in many forms. It may be environmental, caused by adverse weather condition or the remoteness of a location. It may be manmade such as with traffic on a road or electricity in a building. Or it may be a tactical situation. Danger may come from a confused patient or an intoxicated or aggressive bystander.

Slippery or uneven ground can pose a danger to the rescuer, particularly if they rush to help an injured friend then become a casualty themselves. Also before kneeling next to the casualty check the ground next to them for sharp objects and bodily fluids.

As you approach the scene of an incident, you must be constantly aware of (and be continuously reassessing for) potential dangers, and be aware of the casualty and the area around them.

R- Response

After looking for any potential dangers before approaching a casualty, the first Vital Sign we measure is the Patients Level of Response or Level of Consciousness (LOC). This can be measured simply as Conscious or Unconscious or using an extended scale such as the Glasgow Coma Scale (GCS) which is difficult to remember and for beginners can be confusing. A good compromise is to use the AVPU Scale.

A = Awake/ Alert

Alert and oriented to: Time, Date, Place and recent events

V= Responds to voice

Responds appropriately

Confused

Makes incomprehensible sounds (Grunts, groans, etc.)

P= Pain

Response in some way to a pain stimulus

U= Unresponsive

No Response

Anyone who is not Awake & Alert should have their level of consciousness (LOC) monitored and constantly reassessed.

Reason for unconsciousness

There are several common causes of unconsciousness which can be described using the acronym FISHSHAPED;

Fainting,

Intoxication,

Stroke,

Sepsis (infection),

Heart attack,

Shock,

Heat imbalance,

Anaphylaxis,

Poisoning,

Epilepsy and

Diabetes or Dysrythmias (abnormal heart rhythms).

If you attend a patient who is unconscious without a clear history of cause consider all possibilities.

Use of Glasgow Coma Scale should be used to guide the management of head injured patients. The Glasgow Coma Scale is difficult to apply to children under 5 years of age. Although modifications exist, great care needs to be taken with its interpretation. It is especially useful to track changes in conscious state over time. At face value it is easy to use – but you must be literal in the interpretation of each component. Even health care workers commonly misapply it. (See Appendix 1)

S- Shout for help. This applies to normal situations where someone may be close by to assist you, fetch first aid or medical equipment or call for an ambulance.

Primary Assessment

A - Airway:

Secure the airway while taking precautions to stabilise the cervical spine if injury is suspected(see Spinal Immobilisation). Remember airway maintenance is always more important than spinal immobilisation but both should be achieved if possible.

If the casualty is conscious, they will have assumed a position where they can breathe comfortably. Any further interventions must not impair their capacity to breathe.

If the casualty is unconscious, log roll them onto their back and examine their airway. 'Look', 'Listen' and 'Feel' for movement of air.

By placing your left ear near the casualty's mouth you will feel the presence of the breath and will hear any sounds that the breathing produces. If air movement is partially obstructed then the amount of air you feel will be decreased and breathing noisy. Noise on breathing in (*Inspiration*) is indicative of a blockage in the upper respiratory system, whereas noise on breathing out *(Expiration)* indicates a lower blockage. The tongue partially blocking the windpipe may cause a 'snoring' sound or a 'gurgling' sound which would suggest liquid or semi-solid matter such as vomit in the windpipe.

The simplest method of opening the airway is by tilting the head and lifting the chin. This is achieved by pushing the forehead backwards with your left hand whilst supporting the back of the neck. Then place two fingers of your right hand under the tip of the jaw and lift the chin as this will move the tongue from the back of the throat and help clear the airway.

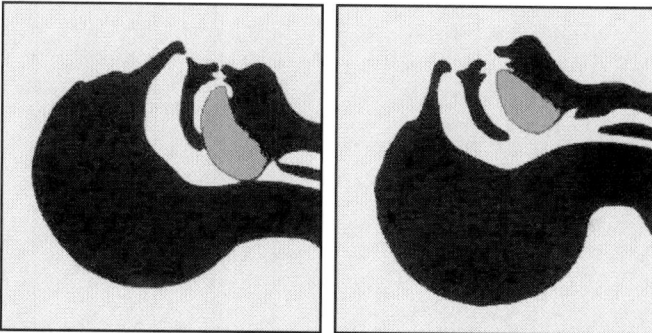

Briefly check mouth for obstructions either from the tongue or the presence of blood, vomit, oedema, loose teeth, dentures or other foreign matter. If you see any debris, sweep your fingers in the casualty's mouth to remove it. Do not sweep blindly as this may increase the obstruction by moving debris further down the airway.

If you have suction equipment or airway adjuncts they can now be used. However if the patent is maintaining their own airway it is often better to avoid unnecessary interventions as these can trigger the gag reflex and cause the patient to choke.

After any airway adjunct has been inserted check if it works by repeating the 'Look', 'Listen', 'Feel' procedure to detect breath sounds and movement.

While examining the airway, check for any smells on the breath such as Alcohol, Cannabis, Pear drops which indicate the presence of Ketones in patients with High blood sugar (hyperglycaemia), Solvents; etc.

A patient who is unable to talk or is hoarse may have swelling, damage or a blockage which could compromise the airway.

B - Breathing:

The assessment of breathing includes providing oxygen and ventilation support if required do not move beyond the breathing stage until this if required is provided.

The acronym RIPPAS can be used to remember the steps needed to fully assess breathing. These are detailed in the section on chest examination.

Rate of Respiration

Inspection for damage or defect in chest wall.

Palpate (feel for injury)

Auscultation (listen for air movement)

Saturations of Oxygen

Once an airway is established; look down the body. If the windpipe is completely blocked but the casualty is still making a respiratory effort then you may still feel and see chest movements, so the presence of breath must be verified. If the blockage is in one of the branches of the windpipe leading into the lungs then chest movement may be uneven.

Observe for a maximum of 10 seconds, in that period you should see and or feel at least two breaths. If breathing is inadequate CPR must be started. This can be achieved by mouth-to-mouth ventilation with or without an airway adjunct or with a bag, valve, mask device (BVM)

RESPIRATION RATE

Is the breathing:

Normal

Normal breathing is regular, un-laboured, quiet and off moderate depth.

Deep

Excessively deep breathing

Shallow

Very small breaths

Laboured

Indicators of laboured breathing are; the patient is leaning forward with hand on knees (tripod Position), nasal flaring, inward movement of the muscles between and below the ribs as a result of reduced pressure in the chest (retractions), using the shoulder, neck and other muscles (accessory muscles) to expand the chest cavity and allow more airflow.

Normal respiration for Adults is *12 - 20 breaths/minute*

Abnormal 10-12 and 20-30 at rest

Serious <10 or >30

Normal Child range varies with age:

30-40 Resps/min newborn – 1 year Old

20-30 Resps/min 2 – 4 years Old

15-20 Resps/min 6 – 12 years Old

12-16 Resps/min at 14 Years Old

Remember: An increased respiration of an injured patient at rest may be the first sign of developing shock.

C - Circulation:

Determine pulse rate and blood pressure (see below) In conditions with serious blood loss, intravenous fluid replacement using saline or blood products is indicated. Only give fluids in the absence of a radial pulse and control the volume given until a pulse is restored.

Control haemorrhaging with direct or indirect pressure; or application of a tourniquet. If circulation is not present; begin CPR or Defibrillation (See Clinical skills).

Capillary Refill Time (CRT)

The CRT is the time it takes blood to return to an area after it has become blanched. CRT can either be measured peripherally on a nail bed, hand or limb. It can also be measured centrally on the chest or forehead

Press on the area for five seconds; it will go pale, then release, if the skin takes more than two seconds to re-colour it indicates reduced circulation. This is an unreliable measure if the patient is cold or already has circulatory problems.

A deficit in the peripheral circulation indicates a circulation problem. A deficit in the central circulation is a serious sign and may be due to shock.

Tissue colour is a good indicator of the state of circulation if you check the inside of the mouth and the lips are pale then the problem is peripheral if the tongue is pale then the problem is central.

Pulse

A pulse needs to be obtained this is usually taken at the radial site in the wrist but can be taken at the neck (carotid pulse) or anywhere an artery crosses over a bone and is close to the skin's surface. Other sites are the groin (femoral), upper arm, between biceps and humerus (brachial pulse), head (temporal), top of foot (dorsalis pedis), back of knee (popliteal). When feeling for a pulse use two or three fingers as the increased surface area will make location easier.

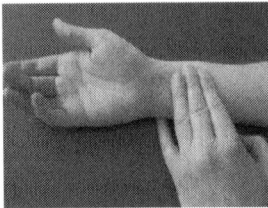

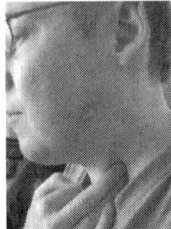

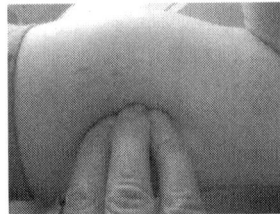

When assessing the Pulse the following should be taken into account:

HEART RATE Either count for 15 Seconds and multiply by 4 or for a full minute.

Average Adult	60-80 Beats/minute
14 Years	80-100 Beats/minute
6 Years - 12 Years	80-120 Beats/minute
2 Years - 4 Years	95-140 Beats/minute
New Born - 1 Year	110-160 Beats/minute

In Adults <60 is Bradycardia (slow pulse) >100 is Tachycardia (fast pulse)

RHYTHM

Regular

Regularly Irregular (With Extra Regular Beats)

Irregularly Irregular (with no discernable pattern, most often a rhythm called Atrial Fibrillation or AF)

QUALITY

Normal, strong and bounding, or weak and thread.

LOCATION

Location is important for three reasons:

Firstly by checking the pulse at the wrist (radial) and the pulse in the neck (carotid) you can roughly guess a blood pressure.

Radial pulse present = B/P $\geq$ 80 systolic

Femoral pulse Present = *B/P $\geq$ 70 systolic*

Carotid pulse present = *B/P $\geq$ 60 systolic*

Although the correlation is inexact, an absent radial pulse means patient is sick, an absent femoral and radial pulse means the patient is very sick.

Secondly, having unequal pulses in two arms may indicate a cardiac problem.

Thirdly, lack of pulses in a limb could indicate damage to the vessels from disease, direct or indirect trauma.

Secondary survey, Action plans and recovery position

E – Exposure / Search

In an unconscious or trauma patient remove clothing (Exposure) and look for additional wounds and any other unseen injuries (bleeding, bruising, burns or deformity). After an area is checked replace clothes or cover with a blanket to prevent heat loss. Check for medical alert bracelets, pendants or cards. Check if they are carrying any medication, a basic knowledge of common prescription medication will give you a good idea of a person's medical history providing of course the medication is theirs.

F – Fahrenheit

After exposing the casualty to check for further injury, care must be taken to preserve body heat (Fahrenheit) whilst performing any procedures required. If you have already started giving IV Fluids this will chill the body unless they have been pre-warmed.

G – Get a Set of Base Vital Signs

When assessing patients it is important to obtain a set of observations, sometimes known as vital signs, this is required for four main reasons;

To aid identification of the underlying problem

To gauge the severity of injury or illness

To monitor the progress of the patient's condition

To assess the effectiveness of treatment on the patient's condition

Vital signs include;

Level of Consciousness (see above)

Pulse (see above)

Respiration Rate (see above)

Blood Pressure (see under clinical skills)

Temperature (see below)

Capillary Refill Time (CRT) (see above)

Skin Colour and Turgor (see below)

Blood Glucose (see under clinical skills)

Oxygen saturations (see under clinical skills)

TEMPERATURE

Normal Temperature range is 36.5 – 37.5 degrees Celsius.

Temperatures can be recorded with glass mercury, disposable paper (temp dot) or digital oral or tympanic (Ear) thermometer. Fever strips are also available to place on the forehead.

Four locations for placement are oral (under tongue), axilla (under armpit), tympanic (ear) or rectal (anus).

Thermometers should be left in place for 3 minutes. Axilla temperatures are generally one degree lower than oral ones.

SKIN COLOUR

Variation in skin colour can be indicate state of circulation and presence of disease;

PINK = Normal

PALE, WHITE, GREY = Can indicate *Shock*

FLUSHED (RED) = Carbon Monoxide, High Blood pressure, Fever

BLUE = Hypoxia (Decreased Oxygen)

YELLOW / JAUNDICE = Liver Injury / Failure, Hepatitis, Cirrhosis

Texture:	Clammy, Wet or Dry
Temperature:	Cold, Warm or Hot

Skin Turgor

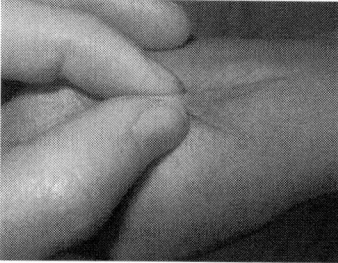

Turgor or tenting is a measure of the elasticity of the skin. It can become reduced if the patient is dehydrated by around 10% or more. Dehydration is often caused by severe diarrhoea and/or vomiting or a decreased fluid intake. Infants and the elderly are most at risk especially those with a fever.

To assess lightly pinch some skin on the back of the hand, forearm or abdomen. Hold for a 5 seconds then release. Normally the skin would snap back to its normal position. If however the patient is dehydrated the skin returns slowly to normal or remains peaked.

H - History

If the patient is conscious ask them what happened, the events, signs and symptoms that led to their current condition. If not and if there were any witnesses to the incident or accident obtain as much information as possible from them. If they know the casualty asks about past incidents, medical history & any current medication or drug allergies. See Medical Assessment below.

Then perform a Head to Toe examination

H - Head-to-Toe Examination

Head to toe examinations are most commonly performed on patients who have been injured in a way that might cause multiple problems, such as falls and road accidents.

Each area of the body should be examined using the DCAPBTLS system looking for the presence of;

(D)eformity, (C)ontusion, (A)brasion, (P)uncture/Penetrating Injury, (B)urns, (T)enderness, (L)aceration & (S)welling

The areas are examined in order of importance; the area's most likely to kill or seriously disable the patient are examined first.

Additionally different areas have specific methods of examination;

Head

Examine the scalp for wounds. Look for blood, fluid or vomit in the mouth, blood or fluid in the ears. Observe for bruising behind the ear ("Battle sign") and bruising around the eyes ("racoon eyes") which may indicate a fracture of the base of the skull.

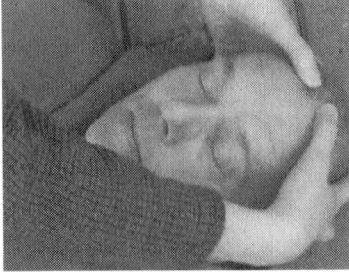

Yellow tinged blood or fluid coming from the nose or ears indicates the presence of cerebral spinal fluid CSF. This fluid encases the brain and its presence in blood indicates a skull fracture.

Whist examining the head recheck the pupil reactions. Look in the eyes and check for redness or a puffy appearance, is there blood or pus present? Are the eyes yellow suggesting the patient is jaundiced.

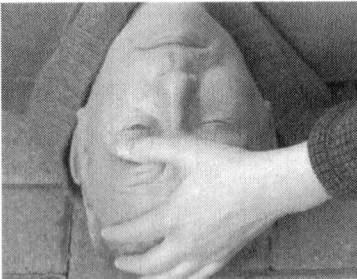

Wounds to the head, face, mouth or neck may suggest possible cervical spine injury.

Check central capillary refill on forehead.

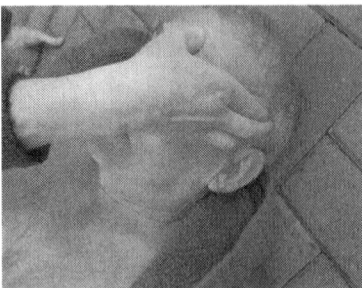

Airway compromise from facial injuries is potentially lethal due to haemorrhage, swelling and debris. Immediate stabilisation of the airway is imperative. Airway patency should be re-evaluated throughout care and transport.

Neck

Distended neck veins may result from a tension pneumothorax (Punctured Lung) or cardiac tamponade (Punctured Heart). Tracheal deviation may indicate a tension pneumothorax although this is a late sign and the patient would be seriously ill at this stage.

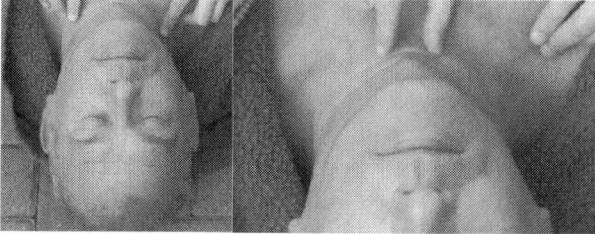

Crumpling cellophane sensation under the skin of the neck may indicate a pneumothorax with subcutaneous emphysema (Air in tissue).

Neck wounds require aggressive airway management due to the potential for rapid deterioration. Intubation should be attempted immediately in an unconscious patient if increasing neck swelling may compromise patient's airway.

Torso

Trunk wounds may consist of damage either to the chest or abdominal cavity.

Chest

Examine the chest using DCAPBTLS see above. Observe for equal and symmetrical chest rise. Place thumbs on breast bone (sternum) and fan fingers out along each side of ribs. Use firm pressure to check for deformities in the chest wall by moving hands down sternum and ribs. When the patient exhales place thumbs tip to tip on their sternum, now as they inhale your thumbs should move apart equally. This will give you an indication of the symmetry and depth of breathing.

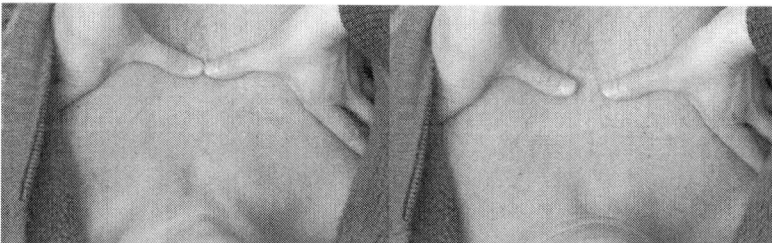

Using a stethoscope listen to the chest for breath sounds (Auscultation). Start at the front (Anterior) of Chest and listen from side to side then move from top to bottom avoid the areas covered by bones

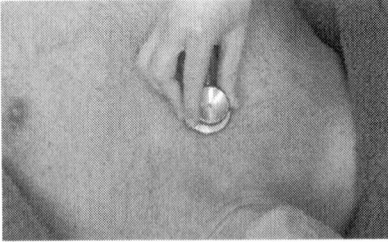

Compare one side to the other looking for differences. Note the location and quality of the sounds you hear.

In a trauma assessment you are primarily concerned with the presence or absence, rate and depth of breathing and noises that indicate a blockage to the airways. You may also hear other sounds these are detailed under respiratory assessment below.

Abdomen

Examine the chest using DCAPBTLS see above.

Feel the abdomen to check for tenderness, distension or rigidity which can indicate damage to organs and internal bleeding. For a more detailed abdominal examination see medical assessment below.

Pelvis

If the pelvis is fractured poor handling can cause significant blood loss. See trauma chapter for more details. Look for signs of incontinence this can indicate spinal damage or seizure activity.

Legs and Arms

Examine the legs first as these contain the larger bones and blood vessels from which patients can lose the most blood. Move on to collar bones, shoulders, arms and hands. When you reach the wrist check for a radial pulse and check peripheral capillary refill at fingers

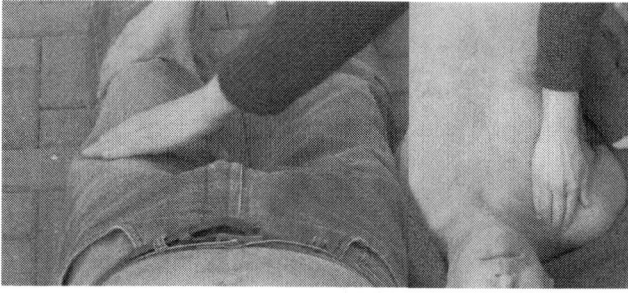

Evaluate extremities using DCAPBTLS.

Then check for Circulation, Sensation and Movement (CSM):

(C)irculation

Is the skin a normal 'Pink' Colour or are extremities pale or cyanosed? Can pulses be felt away (distal) from the site of the injury?

(S)ensation

Can the casualty feel you touching them, is the sensation the same on both sides of the body? If not this can be due to a neurological problem.

(M)ovement

Can the casualty move limbs, fingers and toes? Does pain restrict movement? If not do they have a fracture or muscular injury.

I – Invert ("it's not over until they are over")

Turn the casualty over using a log roll to examine their back. Feel along the spine for irregularities and tenderness.

Taking a Medical History

Using the acronym SAMPLE is a structured way of recording a patient's history. It's not the only way, and perhaps not the best, but provides a good workable system for the lay person.

- Signs and Symptoms
- Allergies
- Medications
- Past Medical History
- Last (Eaten, Bowel Open, Urinated etc)
- Events leading up to current situation

Gathering this information, even in a first aid situation is useful to pass on to the emergency services in the event the patient becomes unconsciousness before they arrive as it gives them clues to the patient's condition and therefore treatment options.

Signs and Symptoms

A Sign is anything you can see, hear, smell or feel that is pertinent to the patient. Typical signs include bleeding, pale skin, deformity of a bone, noisy breathing, smell of alcohol or crepitus etc. A Symptom is anything the patient feels; hot, cold, tired, thirsty, nauseous etc.

Allergies

It is important to note any allergies or drug sensitivities such as Aspirin, Ibuprofen or Penicillin or any other reactions to substances such as latex or plasters as this may alter the treatment a patient receives.

Medication

A list of the patient's medication will give some clues to their medical history. It never ceases to amaze practitioners how many people claim to have very little wrong with them but are taking over a dozen different drugs. These people are either ignorant of why the medication was prescribed to them, trusting in what the doctors tell them, or are in oblivious about their multiple medical problems. Also ask about spray, inhalers, patches and creams as some people don't consider these to be medicine in the same way as tablets. Ask about anything they may have bought from a pharmacy that is not prescribed and if they have taken any 'recreational drugs'.

Past Medical History

A list of pertinent points of interest about the person's past medical history is important to record, the fact that a person has high blood pressure or diabetes is important, the fact they broke their wrist 20 years ago is less so.

Specifically ask about the following using the acronym as a memory aid J THREADS;

J - Jaundice,

T - Tuberculosis,

H – High Blood Pressure, heart attack and disease,

R - Rheumatic fever,

E - Epilepsy,

A - Asthma & Bronchitis,

D - Diabetes,

S - Stroke

Last (Eaten, Bowel Open, Urinated etc)

The recording of when they last ate or drank used to be recorded in case they needed an operation, obviously this depends on circumstance. It is more important with a diabetic patient or someone who is dehydrated. This can also be applied to other symptoms.

Events

The sequence of events that led up to a particular incident can give clues to the cause. For example, if a person is found to be unconscious it's important to know what happened prior to the event. Did they hit their head or fall, did they complain of head or chest pain, have they been drinking and are intoxicated?

If the patient has pain or is short of breath then this can be assessed using either the OPQRSTA or SOCRATES formula.

OPQRSTA

(O)nset

When did the pain start, what were you doing or had been doing before it started.

(P) Provoke, Palliate or Prevent

Does anything bring the pain on (Provoke), lessen (Palliate) or prevent it. Pain that is more intense when taking a deep breath is more likely to be caused by problem with the lungs or the muscles between the ribs (Intercostal). But a patient with a constant central chest pain is more likely to have a heart problem.

(Q)uality

What is the pain like; is it sharp, dull, crushing or tight? Be cautious with this as the patient's idea of what the pain feels like may not fit with a textbook answer. A person may describe both the discomfort caused by a heart attack and asthma as a heavy pain. But others could separately describe them as crushing and tight.

(R)adiation / (R)epeat

Does the pain go anywhere else, both chest and abdominal pain can often spread through to the back, arms, neck and shoulders. In the case of shortness of breath the 'R' for Radiation becomes Repeat i.e. has this happened before and what was the outcome.

(S)everity

How bad is the pain, is it at a constant level or does it come and go. A good measure is to use a Pain score, ask the patient to set a number against the pain

"where zero is no pain and ten is the worst pain they have experienced"

Again this can be subjective but is a good measure to see if treatment is effective. Score the pain at the beginning and after each intervention that could relieve it.

(T)ime

How long and how frequent is the pain, is it continuous or intermeitent.

(A)ssociated Symptoms

Such as nausea or a feeling of doom felt by people having a heart attack.

SOCRATES

(S)ite

Where is the Pain

(O)nset

When did the pain start, what were you doing or had been doing before it started.

(C)haracter

What's the pain like is it sharp, dull, crushing or tight? Be cautious with this as the patient's idea of what the pain feels like may not fit with a textbook answer. A person may describe both the discomfort caused by a heart attack and asthma as a heavy pain. But others could separately describe them as crushing and tight.

(R)adiation

Does the pain go anywhere else, both chest and abdominal pain can often spread through to the back, arms, neck and shoulders. In the case of shortness of breath the 'R' for Radiation becomes Repeat i.e. has this happened before and what was the outcome.

(A)ssociated Symptoms

Such as nausea or a feeling of doom felt by people having a heart attack.

(T)ime,

How long and how frequent is the pain.

(E)xacerbating/relieving factors

Does anything bring the pain on (Exacerbating), lessen (relieving) or prevent it. Pain that is more intense when taking a deep breath is more likely to be caused by problem with the lungs or the muscles between the ribs (Intercostal). But a patient with a constant central chest pain is more likely to have a heart problem.

(S)everity

How bad is the pain, is it at a constant level or does it come and go. A good measure is to use a Pain score, ask the patient to set a number against the pain

"where zero is no pain and ten is the worst pain they have experienced"

Again this can be subjective but is a good measure to see if treatment is effective. Score the pain at the beginning and after each intervention that could relieve it.

Placing Casualty in the Recovery Position

The recovery position is designed to keep the casualty in a neutral position, keeping the airway open, allowing vomit and secretions to drain away and keeping chest off floor to aid breathing. To place a casualty in the recovery position, follow the steps below

Presuming casualty starts on their back.

Remove glasses and check pockets for bulky objects such as keys that would cause discomfort.

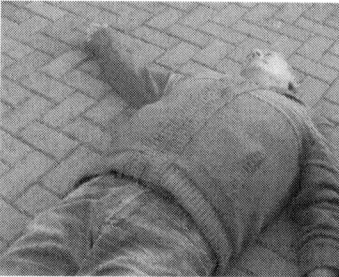

Straighten the casualty's legs then place the arm nearest to you out at right angles to his body, elbow bent with the palm facing up.

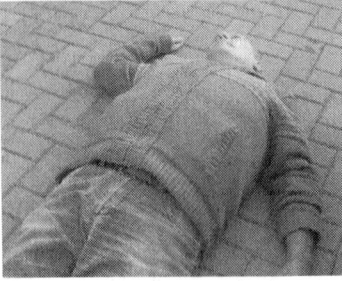

Bring the far arm across the body, whilst holding their hand place it under the cheek nearest to you.

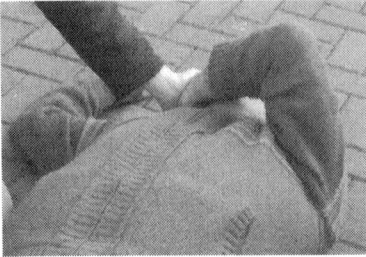

With your other hand, grasp the far leg just above the knee and pull it up, keeping the foot on the ground.

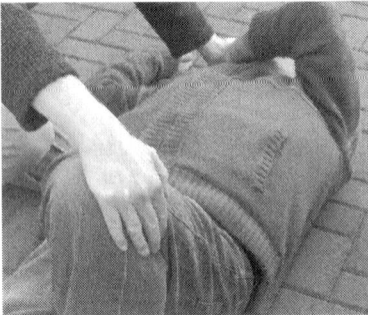

Pull on the far leg to roll the casualty towards you.

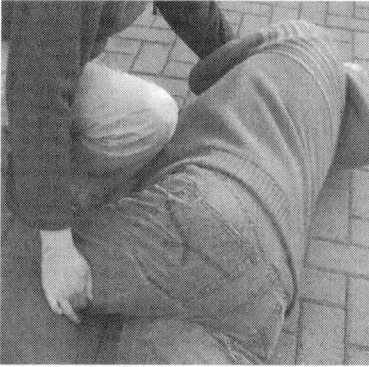

Tilt the head back to maintain a patent airway.

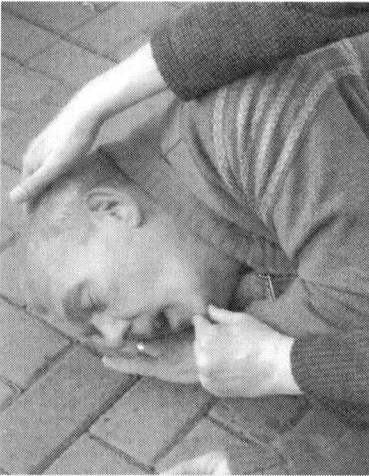

Bend the upper leg so the hip and knee are bent at right angles.

Use back of hand to feel for casualty's breath.

If the casualty remains unconscious for more than 30 minutes roll on other side to prevent pressure areas developing.

Breathing problems

Emphysema

In emphysema, the tissues that support the physical shape of the air sacs (alveoli) in the lungs fail upon exhalation usually due to a long time history of smoking. The main symptoms are shortness of breath (dyspnoea) and a change in the chest as it expands and becomes barrel shaped. Dyspnoea starts on exertion only but can progress so is present all the time to a lesser or greater degree, they use accessory muscles to breathe and will lean forward with arms extended or resting on something to help them breathe called the tripod position, blueness around lips and at finger tips (cyanosis) and their respiratory rate increases. Patient with emphysema are referred to as "pink puffers" who have a pink complexion and shortness of breath.

Bronchitis

Bronchitis is inflammation of the mucous membranes of the bronchi, the airways that carry airflow from the wind pipe (trachea) into the lungs. Bronchitis can acute or chronic;

Acute bronchitis is characterised by the development of a cough, with or without the production of mucus (sputum) that is coughed up. Acute bronchitis often occurs with a viral illness.

In Chronic bronchitis the patient has a productive cough that lasts for three months or more per year for at least two years, caused by smoking, pollution or industrial irritants. They are sometimes called "Blue Bloaters" because of the bluish colour of the skin and lips caused by cyanosis.

Treatment

Encourage patient to sit up which will improve breathing and to take their own medication. If oxygen is available administer it to keep their saturations between 88% and 92% see section on oxygen therapy.

Croup

This is a breathing problem most commonly seen in children between 6 months and 5–6 years of age that is caused by an infection of the upper airway causing swelling inside the throat which in turn causes the classic "barking" seal like cough. Other symptoms are a grating upper airway sound (Stridor), hoarseness, difficulty in breathing, fever, runny nose and drooling. Symptoms vary in intensity and can be worse at night. Normally treated by GP but in rare cases can be very serious.

Manage a choking casualty

Choking can be variable and we generally see two types: mild and severe. Ask the casualty if they are choking, if they can answer then the choking is mild; if not and they nod, point to or grasp their neck it is severe.

Mild Choking

In mild choking the casualty feels something in their throat but is still able to cough, speak and most importantly breathe. In most cases just encourage the casualty to cough and this will clear the obstruction.

Severe Choking

In severe choking the casualty feels something in their throat is unable to cough, speak or breathe. They may have an audible wheeze or be unconscious.

If the casualty is unconscious or becomes so during treatment and there is no signs of breathing start CPR see below.

If they are conscious alternate 5 backslaps with 5 abdominal thrusts. Check after each slap or thrust to see if condition has improved, if the casualty is able to breathe stop and encourage them to cough as above.

To administer back slaps;

Stand behind the casualty.

Support the casualty's torso with one arm and lean the casualty forwards as far as comfortable

Give up to 5 blows between the shoulder blades with the heel of your hand.

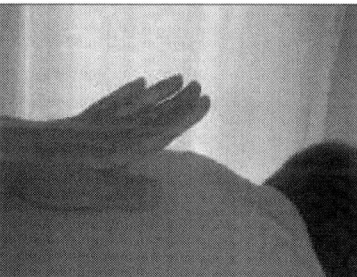

To administer abdominal thrusts;

Stand behind casualty and put both arms round their abdomen. Lean the casualty forwards.

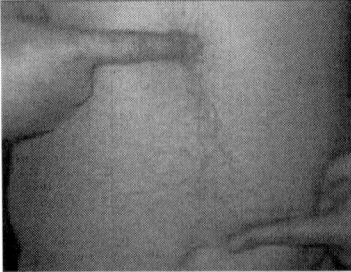

Clench your fist and place it between the navel and the bottom of the breastbone (sternum).

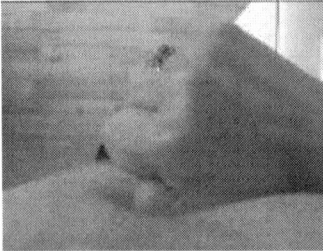

Grasp this hand with your other hand and pull sharply inwards and upwards with a rolling motion.

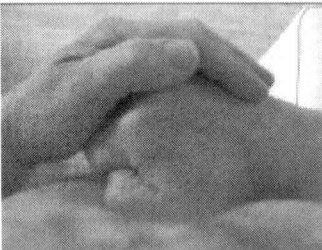

Repeat up to five times.

Anaphylaxis & Epi-pen

A mild allergic reaction often causes no more symptoms than an itchy rash, this is not serious in itself, and may be treated with oral or topical antihistamines and cold showers / wet flannels. If difficulty in breathing or swallowing develops, and/or a sudden weakness regard these as serious symptoms requiring immediate treatment see below. Allergic diseases are on a spectrum with a mild rash at one end and life threatening anaphylaxis at the other.

Anaphylaxis

Anaphylaxis is caused by exposure to an antigen which triggers a cascading release of mediators (such as histamine). Causing the blood vessels to become leaky and inappropriately expanding (Dilation).

Anaphylaxis is potentially life threatening and requires prompt treatment to prevent deterioration and death. Its key features which differentiate it from an allergic reaction are;

Airway swelling

Airway constriction

Low blood pressure

Altered level of consciousness

A sudden onset

Wheeze and/or Stridor (see chapter 1)

It can be caused by insect stings, particularly wasp and bee stings. Certain foods such as eggs, fish, cow's milk protein, peanuts, nuts and drugs including blood products, vaccines, antibiotics and aspirin.

If using any medication it is a wise precaution to prepare for Anaphylactic reactions.

Treatment

Maintain airway

Maintain blood pressure (lay flat, raising the feet)

Administer adrenaline

Give an antihistamine

Give Nebulised Salbutamol & Oxygen

If using a vial of Adrenaline give 0.5mg intramuscularly (IM) or 0.3mg from an auto injector. The dose is repeated if necessary at 5-minute intervals.

If the patient show signs of poor perfusion or shock, intravenous fluids can be given in addition to the adrenaline.

An antihistamine e.g. Piriton can be given orally or by slow intravenous injection of 10mg. This should only be used once the acute phase of the anaphylaxis is over as the antihistamine may worsen any hypotension (low blood pressure)

An intravenous corticosteroid e.g. Hydrocortisone in a dose of 200 mg can also be given but takes around 6 hours to take effect.

Age Dose Volume of adrenaline

(1 in 1000 (1 mg/ml)

Under 6 months 50 micrograms 0.05 ml

6 months–6 years 120 micrograms 0.12 ml

6–12 years 250 micrograms 0.25 ml

Adult and adolescent 500 micrograms 0.5 ml

The doses may be repeated several times if necessary at 5-minute intervals according to blood pressure, pulse and respiratory function.

Adrenaline acts quickly to constrict blood vessels, relax smooth muscles in the airways and improves breathing, it also stimulates the pulse.

Instructions for the administration of adrenaline via the EpiPen® Injector

Grasp EpiPen® in dominant hand, with thumb closest to grey safety cap With the other hand, pull off grey safety cap.

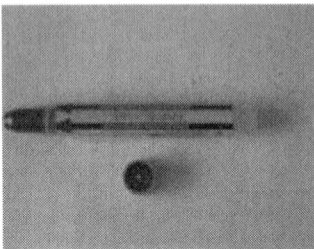

Hold EpiPen® approximately 10cm away from thigh.

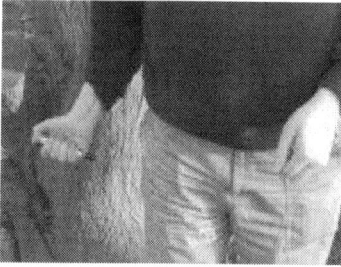

Black tip should point towards outer thigh

Jab firmly into outer thigh so that EpiPen® is at a right angle to outer thigh, through clothing if necessary

Hold in place for 10 seconds.

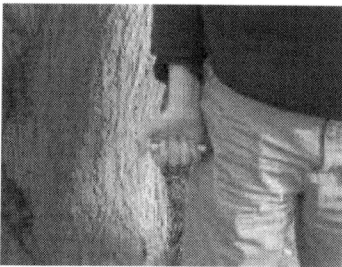

EpiPen® should be removed and handed to team taking over management of the patient if applicable.

Massage injection area for 10 seconds

Patient must be supervised because relapse can occur within a few hours and/or further management may be required

Do not

Use EpiPen® to practise emergency administration

Remove grey safety cap until ready to use EpiPen®

Place fingers over the black tip

Attempt to inject into vein or buttocks

Inject into extremities, as adrenaline causes blood vessels to constrict (Vasoconstriction).

Manage a casualty who is having an asthma attack.

Asthma

Asthma is a disease that affects the lower airways. It is usually triggered by an allergen although a viral respiratory infection, exercise or cold weather may precipitate it. It is part of the "atopy" (allergy) triad of eczema, hay fever and asthma. It manifests as an obstruction of the airways which is caused by a combination of swelling of mucosa and smooth muscle spasm of the small airway muscles causing them to contract and an increase in mucous production that blocks the narrowed airways. It is a common disease affecting over 10% of the population.

Signs and symptoms include shortness of breath (dyspnoea), increased respiration rate, productive cough and an audible wheeze. In children it may present as night-time (nocturnal) coughing.

Mild and moderate asthma presents with shortness of breath and chest tightness, plus sign of increased use of the chest wall muscles (the accessory muscles) to help with breathing and a slight reduction in sentence length and the presence of a wheeze when listening to the chest (Auscultation).

As it gets worse (severe to life threatening asthma) the patient will not be able to speak in full sentences, pulse may be >110/min, the respiratory rate >25/min, they may also start using the accessory muscles in the neck and shoulders. In life threatening asthma, no air movement and no wheeze can be heard when listening to the chest, the patient's extremities become blue-tinged (Cyanosed), their pulse rate drops (Bradycardia) and they become exhausted as breathing becomes more difficult.

Peak Flow Measurement

Peak flow is often used as a measure to further define the severity of an asthma attack. It relies on a patient being able to accurately undertake the measurement.

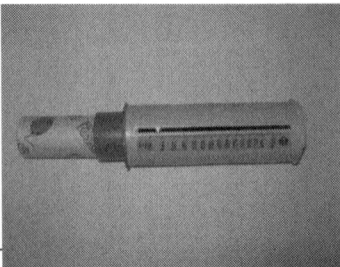

1/Zero the pointer on the scale
2/Breathe in as fully as possible.
3/Blow out as hard and fast as possible.
4/Repeat this sequence twice more.
5/The highest of the three readings is your peak flow.

A person having a serious asthma attack will struggle to blow into the Peak flow meter.

Although it is a good baseline measurement for treatment be aware of this.

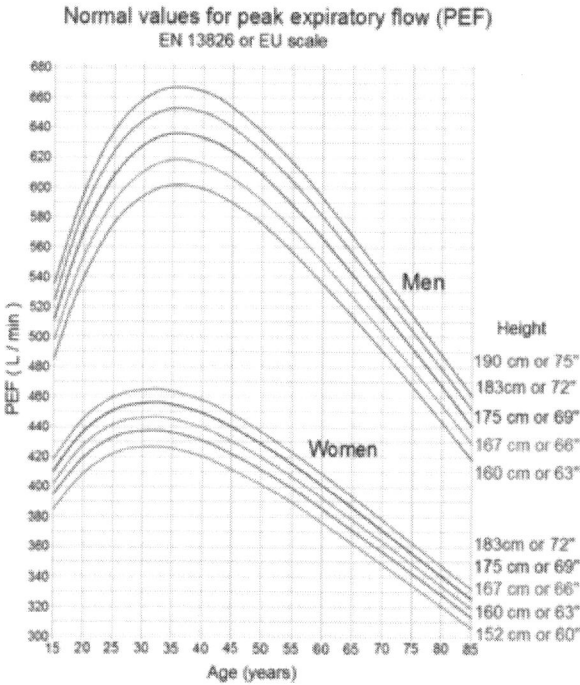

Normal values for peak expiratory flow (PEF)
EN 13826 or EU scale

Nunn A, Gregg I (1989). "New regression equations for predicting peak expiratory flow in adults". *BMJ* 298 (6680): 1068–70.

Normal	80-100 % of Predicted Score
Mild Attack	51-79 % of Predicted Score
Severe Attack	33-50 % Predicted Score
Life Threatening	<33 % of Predicted Score

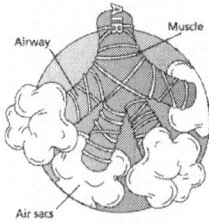

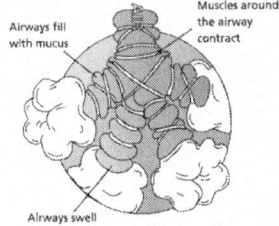

Treatment

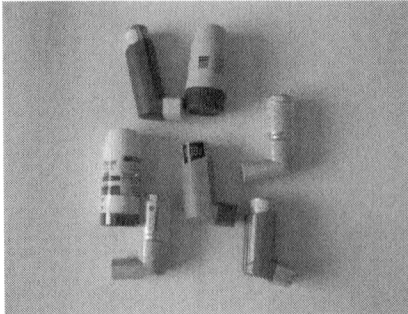

Asthmatics generally use one or more inhalers and possibly nebulised drugs to manage their condition. Inhalers come in all colours, shapes and sizes, containing different drugs. The drugs fall into two sorts 'preventers' for keeping airways open usually taken at set periods throughout the day and 'relievers' to open the airways when the chest becomes tight or the patient has an asthma attack. The most common inhaler in use is the blue Ventolin inhaler containing the drug Salbutamol used to relieve attacks each puff delivers 0.4mg.

Technique for spacers

A volumetric spacer is a way to more effectively use an asthma inhaler. Essentially it is a small breathing chamber that the drug from the inhaler is shot into and then breathed in and out by the patient, it is more effective than using the inhaler alone.

For each puff have the patient take 10 deep breaths before giving a second puff.

Maintenance treatment

> 2 puffs twice a day via the spacer

Acute treatment

10 puffs as required via a spacer – equivalent to a 5mg nebuliser.

In patients with mild to moderate asthma spacers are just as effective as nebulisers. Provided the patient is awake and cooperative it is likely to be just as effective in severe to life threatening asthma.

A spacer can easily be improvised using a 600 ml or 1.25L coke type bottle. Cut ½ a dozen 1cm² holes into the bottom of the bottle and a slightly larger one for the size of the inhaler mouth piece. The patient can breathe through the mouth of the bottle the same way as with the spacer.

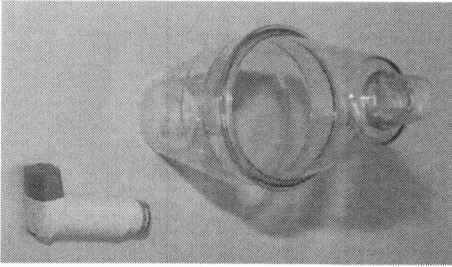

©Tradimus

Technique for Nebulising

It can be administered via a machine on air or via oxygen from a cylinder. If used on oxygen set the cylinder to deliver 6-8 litres using the dial on top. This is enough to nebulise the medication.

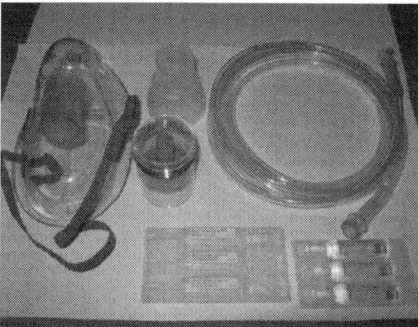

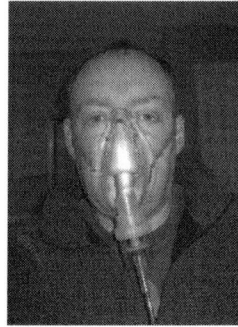

The nebuliser kit consists of a facemask, a two part chamber where the drug is held and oxygen tubing. The drug is placed in the lower chamber and the two halves are screwed together. The mask fits in the top and the tubing in the bottom. Ensure mask fits tightly to patients face. Drugs for use with a nebuliser are usually supplied in plastic ampoules.

The two common drugs used are;

Salbutamol supplied in (2.5mg /5mg) Ampoules

Atrovent supplied in (400mcg) Ampoules

In severe asthma the;

First dose is 5mg Salbutamol

Second dose is 5mg Salbutamol + 400mcg Atrovent

Third + doses is 5mg Salbutamol

Before an Asthma Episode

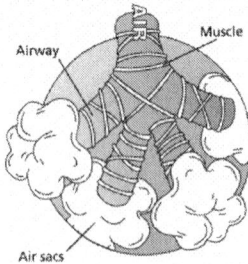

Muscle

Airway

Air sacs

After an Asthma Episode

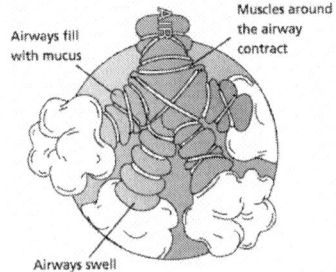

Airways fill
with mucus

Muscles around
the airway
contract

Airways swell

Chronic asthma

If possible the patient should be commenced on a preventer (usually steroid) inhaler, which reduces the swelling and inflammation in the airways.

Hyperventilation

Breathing faster and or deeper than normal is called hyperventilation tis causes loss of carbon dioxide. It is usually caused by an anxiety episode but should not be dismissed as it can also be caused by some diseases and head injuries.

Symptoms such as numbness or tingling in the hands, feet and lips, dizziness, headache, chest pain, slurred speech, nervous laughter, and sometimes fainting. If the patient faints their breathing usually resets.

Basic Life Support (BLS)

Cardio Pulmonary Resuscitation (CPR)

BLS is to buy time for defibrillation and or advanced care, where the patient is in a shockable rhythm. Exceptions to this include electrocution, drowning or asthma where the cause of the collapse may be due to a respiratory problem and CPR alone may be of value.

Information below based on the 2010 Resuscitation Guidelines. This can be divided into Basic (BLS), Intermediate (ILS) and Advanced Life Support (ALS);

CPR Aids

Basic aids such as resuscitation face shields and pocket masks are widely available to assist in delivering CPR and provide a barrier between

Adult Basic Life Support (BLS)

- Check for Danger
- Check for Catastrophic Bleeding
- Check for Response (AVPU)
- Shout/Call for Help
- Place patient on back

Airway

- Check Airway is Clear; clear if not
- Open the patient's airway by placing one hand on their head to tilt it back and two fingers of the other hand, under their chin to lift the jaw. Consider using a Jaw Thrust If they are likely to have a neck injury. Remember without an Airway, Breathing and circulation will soon cease

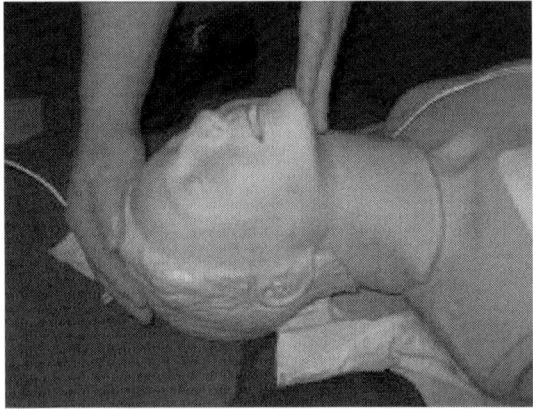

Breathing

- Check breathing maximum of 10 seconds, by placing your ear close to the casualty's mouth and looking down the chest. You will be able to see the chest rise, feel breath on your cheek and may hear sounds of breathing.
- If less than two good breathes are heard within 10 seconds start CPR

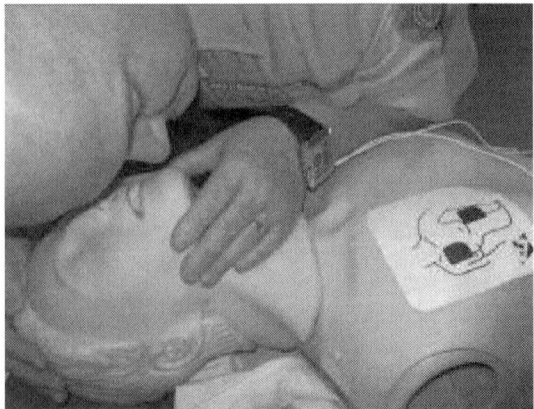

Circulation

- Check for signs of Circulation such as coughing, opening his eyes, speaking or moving purposefully

Place two hands on the centre of the chest, one on top of each other, lean over the patient's chest so your hands are straight.

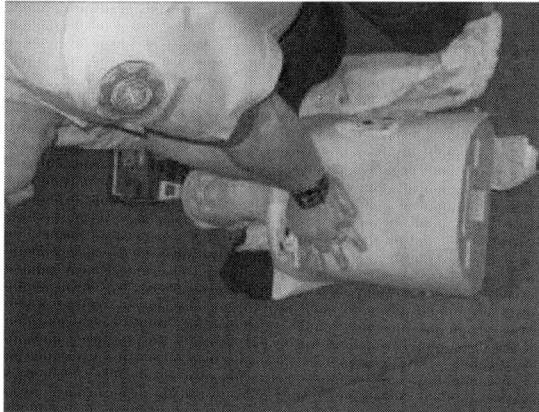

Give 30 Compressions (depressing the chest 5-6 cms) at a rate of 100-120/min

- Give 2 Rescue Breathes, each breath lasting 1 second.

- Repeat giving 30 compressions and 2 rescue breaths.

Do not stop to check the victim or discontinue CPR unless the victim starts to show signs of regaining consciousness, such as coughing, opening his eyes, speaking or moving purposefully AND starts to breathe normally.

Pediatrics CPR (Children below 12 years of Age)

- Check for Danger
- Check for Catastrophic Bleeding
- Check for Response (AVPU)
- Shout/Call for Help
- Place patient on back

Airway

- Check Airway is Clear; clear if not

Children > 1 year

- Open the patient's airway by placing one hand on their head to tilt it back and two fingers of the other hand, under their chin to lift the jaw. Consider using a Jaw Thrust If they are likely to have a neck injury.

Children < 1 year

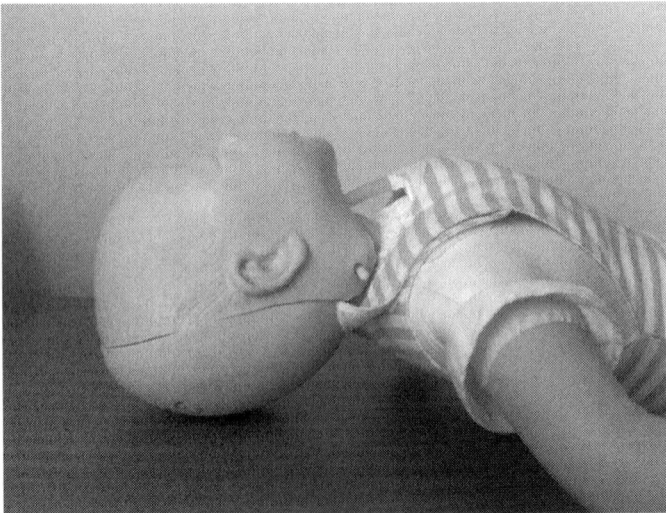

Open the patient's airway by moving their head back into a neutral position this may require placing something under their shoulders to offset the size of the back of their head.

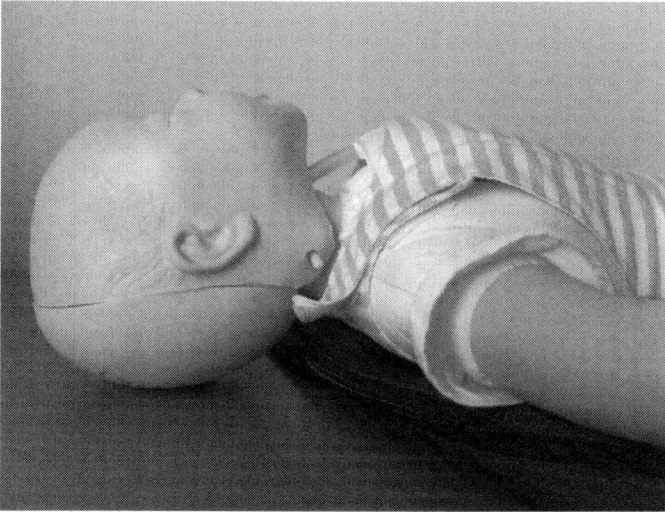

Remember without an airway, breathing and circulation will soon cease

Breathing

- Check breathing maximum of 10 seconds, by placing your ear close to the casualty's mouth and looking down the chest. You will be able to see the chest rise, feel breath on your cheek and may hear sounds of breathing.

Circulation

- Check for signs of Circulation such as coughing, opening his eyes, speaking or moving purposefully

If no breathing or signs of circulation commence CPR as below;

- Give 5 rescue breathes each

- Recheck Breathing and Circulation for 10 seconds if adequate place child in recovery position if not continue with CPR

For children 1-11 place one hand, 1 finger width above the end of their breast bone (sternum)

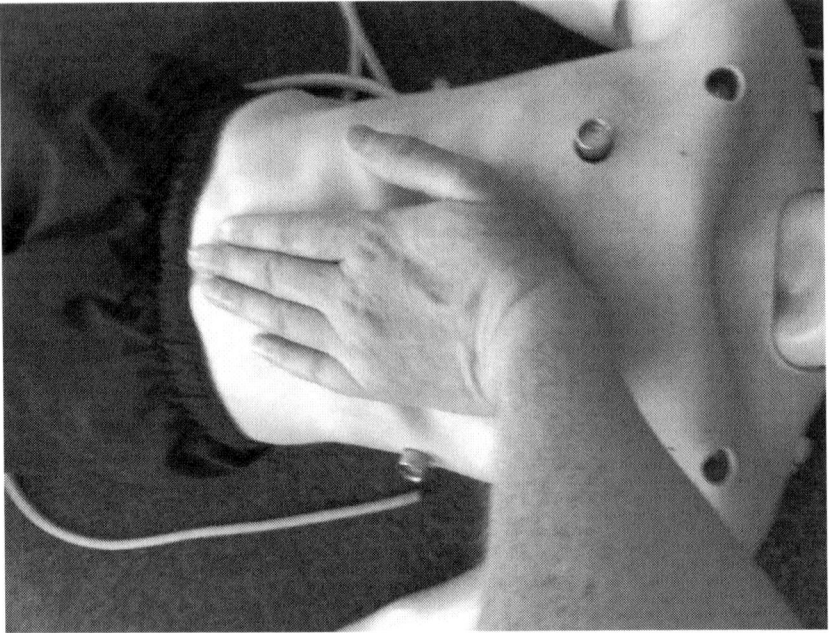

For infants place two fingers, 1 finger width above the end of their breast bone (sternum)

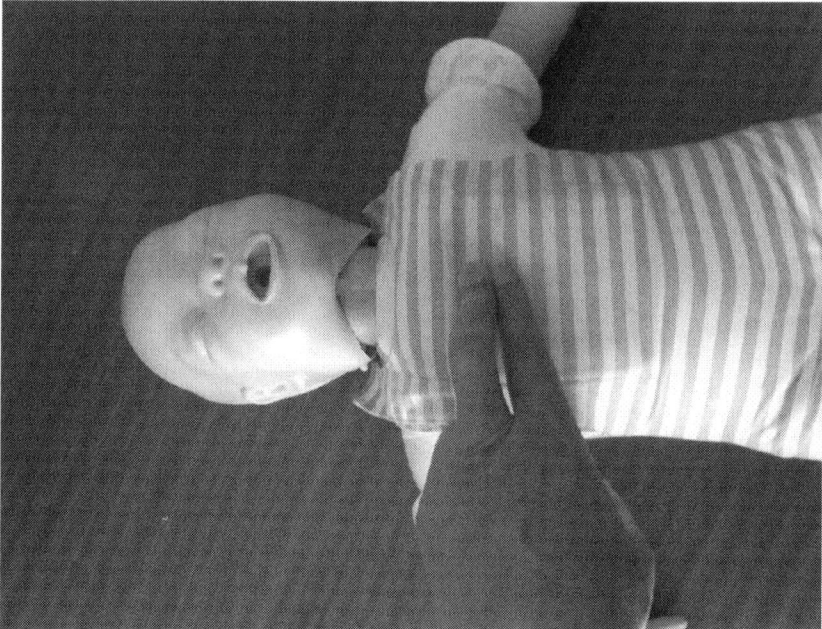

- Give 30 Compressions (depressing the chest 1/3 of its depth) at a rate of 100-120/min

- Give 2 Rescue Breathes, each breath lasting 1 second.

- Repeat giving 30 compressions and 2 rescue breaths.

Do not stop to check the victim or discontinue CPR unless the victim starts to show signs of regaining consciousness, such as coughing, opening his eyes, speaking or moving purposefully AND starts to breathe normally.

Intermediate Life Support (ILS)
Is Basic Life support with the addition of resuscitation equipment such as;

- Automatic External Defibrillator,
- Oropharyngeal airways (OPA),
- Nasopharyngeal airways (NPA),
- Bag-valve-mask (BVM),
- Supplementary oxygen,

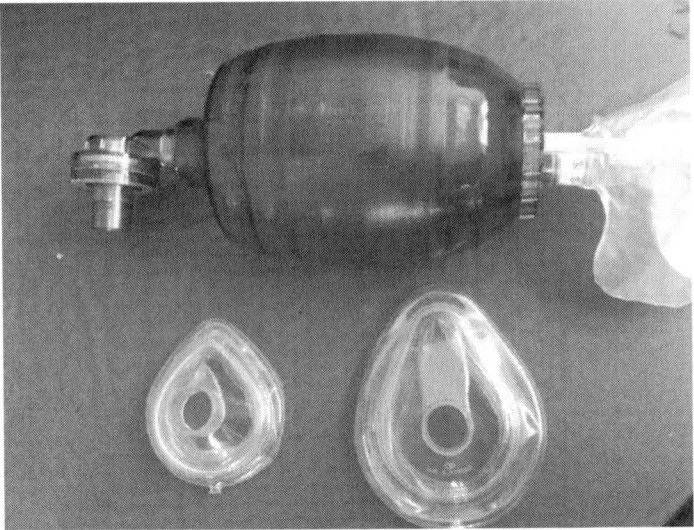
Adult BVM with child and adult masks

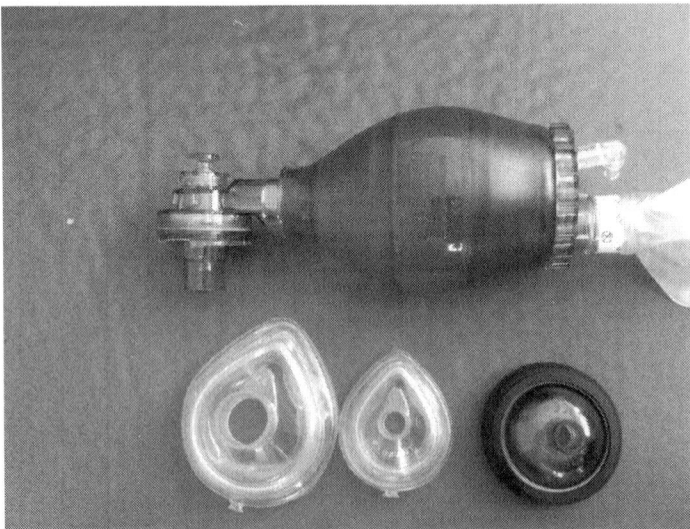
Child BVM with Child and two infant masks

With the exception of an AED these should only be used if you are trained to use them

Manage a casualty with shock

If you've ever injured yourself significantly (or given blood) in addition to the pain you may have experienced being weak, dizzy, and nauseous, in which case you may have experienced a mild form of shock. In this case, the symptoms appeared immediately after the injury, but they may not show up for several hours dependant on the speed of the blood or fluid loss. Shock is a condition in which blood circulation is seriously disturbed. Crushed or fractured bones, burns, prolonged bleeding, asphyxia and dehydration can all cause Shock.

Shock may be slight or it may be severe enough to be fatal. Because all traumatic injuries result in some form of shock, you should learn its symptoms and know how to treat the casualty.

The best approach to Shock Prevention is to treat all casualties suffering from moderate and severe injuries for shock even if they are no showing immediate signs or symptoms.

Shock is defined as widespread poor blood supply (hypo-perfusion) of the tissues and cells resulting in not enough oxygen and nutrients arriving at the various parts of the body and not enough waste products produced in the cells is being removed. The organ that needs the best perfusion is the brain.

Shock is frequently the most serious consequence of an injury

Types of Shock

Shock can be caused by several different processes and a useful analogy is to consider the human vascular system as a houses heating system consisting of a pump (Heart) and pipes /heating circuit (Vessels) and radiators (Organs):

• Hypovolemic shock - (losing the fluid from the pipes)

There are several causes:

Haemorrhagic – loss of blood due to either internal or external bleeding.

Intestinal obstruction - results in the movement of large amount of plasma from the blood into the intestine.

Severe burns - loss of large amounts of plasma from the burned surface.

Dehydration results from severe and prolonged shortage of water intake.

Severe diarrhoea or vomiting - loss of plasma through the intestinal wall.

- Distributive shock: (dilation of the pipes) through either nerves (neurogenic shock) or local chemicals (anaphylactic or septic shock) causes the blood vessels to dilate or become leaky.

Neurogenic shock through a spinal cord injury causes rapid loss of contractibility of blood vessels (Vasomotor Tone) that leads to them expanding (Vasodilatation) to the extent that a severe decrease in blood pressure results. Anaesthesia also decreases the activity of the area of the brain that controls constriction and dilation of blood vessels (*medullary vasomotor*).

Anaphylactic shock - results from an allergic response that causes the release of inflammatory substances that increase vasodilatation and amount of leakage (Capillary Permeability).

Septic shock or "blood poisoning" - results from peritoneal, systemic, and gangrenous infections that cause the release of toxic substances into the circulatory system, depressing the activity of the heart, leading to vasodilatation, and increasing the amount of leakage (Capillary Permeability).

- Cardiogenic shock - (the pump itself is broken): Occurs when the heart stops pumping or performance is decreased in response to conditions such as a heart attack or a very rapid heart rate.

How to recognise Shock

A person who is going into shock may show quite a few different signs or symptoms, some of which are indicated below and are discussed in the following paragraphs. They reflect the effect of the poor blood supply (perfusion) or the various ways the body has to compensate for this poor blood flow. Remember that some signs of shock do not always appear at the time of the injury; and, in some very serious cases the symptoms may not appear until hours later. Shock is caused directly or indirectly, by the disturbance of the circulation of the blood. Symptoms of shock include the following:

- The pulse is weak and rapid.
- Breathing is likely to be shallow, rapid, and irregular, because the poor circulation of the blood affects the breathing centre in the brain.
- The temperature near the surface of the body is lowered because of the poor blood flow; so the face, arms, and legs feel cold to the touch.
- Sweating is likely to be very noticeable.

- A person in shock is usually very pale, but, in some cases, the skin may have a bluish or reddish colour. In the case of victims with dark skin, you may have to rely primarily on the colour of the mucous membranes on the inside of the mouth or under the eyelid or under the nail bed. A person in or going into shock has a bluish colour to these membranes instead of a healthy pink.

- The pupils of the eyes are usually dilated (enlarged).

- If the casualty is conscious, they may complain of thirst. They may have a feeling of weakness, faintness, or dizziness, or they may feel nauseous.

- The casualty may be very restless and feel frightened and anxious. As shock deepens, these signs gradually disappear and the victim becomes increasingly unresponsive to what is going on around them. Even pain may not arouse them. Finally, the victim may become deeply unconscious.

© Lev Olkha | Dreamstime.com

You are unlikely to see all the symptoms of shock in any one case. Some symptoms may appear only in later stages of shock when the disturbance of the blood flow has become so great that the person's life is in serious danger. Sometimes other signs of the injury may disguise the signs of shock. You must recognise which symptoms indicate the presence of shock, but do not ever wait for symptoms to develop before beginning the treatment for shock.

Remember, every seriously injured person is likely to develop serious shock!

Prevention and Treatment of Shock

The first priority in the treatment of shock is to stop the underlying cause – stop the blood loss, treat the allergic reaction or severe infection.

You should begin treatment for shock as soon as possible. Prompt treatment may prevent the onset of shock or, if it has already developed, prevent it reaching a critical point. Keep the victim lying down and warm. If conscious, the victim should be encouraged and depending on the circumstances assure that expert medical help will arrive soon.

Keep an injured person warm enough for comfort, but do not let the victim become overheated.

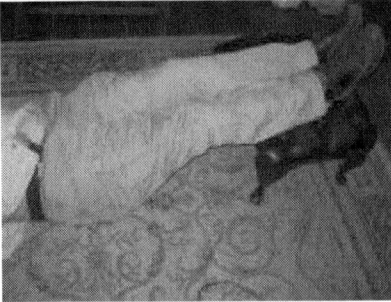

The best position to use to reduce the onset or to help in the treatment of shock is one that encourages the flow of blood to the brain. If possible, place the injured person on their back on either the floor, a bed, cot, or stretcher. Raise the lower end of the support about 12 inches so that the feet are higher than the head. If this is not possible, raise the feet and legs enough to help the blood flow to the brain. Sometimes it may be possible to take advantage of a natural slope and place the victim so that the head is lower than the feet.

Of course every case is different and you will have to consider the type of injury before you can decide on the best position for the patient. Here are some examples:

• If a person has a chest wound, they may have so much trouble breathing that you will have to raise the head slightly.

• If the face is flushed, rather than pale, or if you have any reason to suspect a head injury, do not raise the feet. Instead, you should keep the head level with or slightly higher than the feet.

• If the person has broken bones, you will have to judge what position would be best both for the fractures and for shock. A fractured spine must be immobilised before the victim is moved at all, if further injuries are to be avoided.

It is often useful to ask the patient to adopt the position which is most comfortable for them. If you have any doubts about the correct position to use, have the victim lie flat on their back. The basic position for treating shock is one in which the head is lower than the feet. Do the best you can under the particular circumstances, to get the injured person into this position. NEVER let a seriously injured person sit, stand, or walk around.

No particular harm will be done if you allow the victim to moisten their mouth and lips with cool water, if it will make them more comfortable. Administer liquids sparingly and not at all if medical attention will be available within a short time. If necessary, small amounts of warm water, tea, or coffee may be given to a victim who is conscious. Persons having serious burns are an exception. Burn victims require large amounts of fluids. Water, tea, fruit juices, and sugar water may be given freely to a victim who is conscious, able to swallow, and has no internal injuries. Slightly salted water is also beneficial. This should be done if they are fully conscious, able to swallow, and you do not suspect that they have suffered internal injuries. Never give alcohol to a person in shock, as this will cause blood vessels to dilate and reduce blood pressure.

An injured person may or may not be in pain. The amount of pain felt depends in part on the person's physical condition and the type of injury. Extreme pain, if not relieved, can increase the degree of shock. Make the victim as comfortable as possible. Fractures should be immobilised and supported. Immobilisation greatly reduces, and sometimes eliminates, pain.

An injured person's body heat must be conserved. Therefore, warmth is important in the treatment of shock. Exposure to cold, with resulting loss of body heat, can cause shock to develop or to become worse. You will have to judge the amount of covering to use by considering the weather and the general circumstances of the accident.

Often a light covering will be enough to keep the casualty comfortable. Wet clothing should be removed and dry covering provided, even on a hot day. Use blankets or any dry material to conserve body heat. Artificial means of warming (hot water bottles, heated bricks, heated sand) should not ordinarily be used. Artificial heat may cause loss of body fluids (by sweating, and it brings the blood closer to the surface, defeating the body's own efforts to supply blood to the vital organs and to the brain. Also, the warming agent may burn the victim.

The treatment of Shock. In many emergency situations, is the most helpful thing you can do for an injured person. If shock has not yet developed, the treatment may actually prevent its occurrence; if it has developed, you may be able to keep it from reaching a critical point.

Emotional Shock

Emotional shock (Faint) – is not shock in the true sense of the work. Sometimes strong emotions can cause strong parasympathetic stimulation of the heart and results in vasodilatation in skeletal muscles and in the viscera.

The impact of this type of shock will vary widely – sometimes there will be a powerful sympathetic nervous system response or times it may just present and anxiety. Comfort and reassurance coupled with rest and relaxation after you are clear of immediate dangers is very effective in management of the casualty suffering from emotional shock. It is important to keep the victim as calm as possible. Try to prevent the victim from seeing their injuries, or others and reassure them that they will be properly cared for. Keep all unnecessary persons away, as their conversation regarding the victim's injuries may increase their agitation.

Clinical Signs of Shock

	Class 1	Class 2	Class 3	Class 4
Blood Loss Volume (mills) in adult	750mls	800 - 1500mls	1500 - 2000mls	>2000mls
Blood Loss % Circ. blood volume	<15%	15 - 30%	30 - 40%	>40%
Systolic Blood Pressure	No change	Normal	Reduced	Very low
Diastolic Blood Pressure	No change	Raised	Reduced	Very low / Unrecordable
Pulse (beats /min)	Slight tachycardia	100 - 120	120 (thready)	>120 (very thready)
Capillary Refill	Normal	Slow (>2s)	Slow (>2s)	Undetectable
Respiratory Rate	Normal	Normal	Raised (>20/min)	Raised (>20/min)
Urine Flow (mills/hr)	>30	20 - 30	10 - 20	0 - 10
Extremities	Normal	Pale	Pale	Pale & cold
Complexion	Normal	Pale	Pale	Ashen
Mental state	Alert, thirsty	Anxious or aggressive, thirsty	Anxious or aggressive or drowsy	Drowsy, confused or unconscious

Fluid Loss (Hypovolaemic) Shock in Children

Signs	<25% Blood Loss	25-40% Blood Loss	>40% Blood Loss
Heart Rate	Increased	Increased	Increased or Reduced
Systolic BP	Normal	Normal or Reduced	Reduced ++
Pulse Volume	Normal or Reduced	Reduced	Reduced ++
Cap Refill	Normal or /ncreased	Increased	Increased
Resp Rate	Increased	Increased	Sighing
Skin Temp	Cool	Cold	Cold
Skin Colour	Pale	Mottled	White/Grey
Mental State	Mild agitation	Drowsy	Reacts to pain only

Remember: A child with >25% shock needs blood & urgent hospital care

Managing a patient with chest pain

Chest pain

This is a very common presenting complaint and is an absolute mine field. Trivial and life threatening can look exactly the same. The pain needs to be put in context:

Trauma vs. not

Age. Young vs. old

 Heart attacks are less common in young people

Sex

Type of pain

Associated symptoms

Types of pain: There are broadly three types of pain:

Pleuritic usually from an irritation of the lungs such as pneumonia, pulmonary embolism. Described as sharp, worse with inspiration and often pain is felt as a "catch".

Visceral pain is more diffuse and harder to localise. Associated with damage or irritation of the heart, oesophagus or gut. Felt as a pressure, sweating and nausea and/or vomiting. It often radiates into the neck, arms and/or back.

Musculoskeletal where the patient describes pain like a pulled muscle, worse with movement. Often the pain is sharp and well localised. There are some similarities to pleuritic pain.

Heart Pain

The heart is a pump. It requires oxygen to work. If it doesn't get enough oxygen it causes visceral pain.

The more activity the person does the more work for heart. The more work the more oxygen is required. Heart disease is the narrowing of blood vessels supplying the heart muscle caused by the build up of fatty deposits.

If the pain occurs during exercise and is relieved by rest its usually caused by Angina this can be stable occurs at same level of exercise or unstable occurs with progressively less exercise. Patients with very unstable angina are treated the same as a heart attack.

If the pain occurs at rest it is usually caused by an obstruction of blood flow, such as caused by a Heart Attack (Myocardial Infarction).

Heart Attack (Myocardial infarction) (MI)

If the blocked blood vessel is small and only supplies a small non vital area, the patient may recover without any treatment and only minimal effect. If however the blockage occurs towards the beginning of one of the main arteries supplying blood to the heart, it's more likely to cause significant damage. The larger the area of damaged heart the more likely it is to produce a lethal heart rhythm and for the patient to die. Most heart attacks occur between these two extremes. See below for a diagram of the heart showing the system of coronary circulation and plaque formation where a build up of cholesterol blocks (Occludes) the vessel.

The problem with heart disease is that a minority of patients present with the "classic" presentation of crushing central chest pain radiating to the neck and arm. The remainder may present with sharp musculoskeletal type pain or indigestion or even jaw or arm pain in isolation. Some patients will not experience any pain, which is more common amongst those that have diabetes due to degradation of nerves.

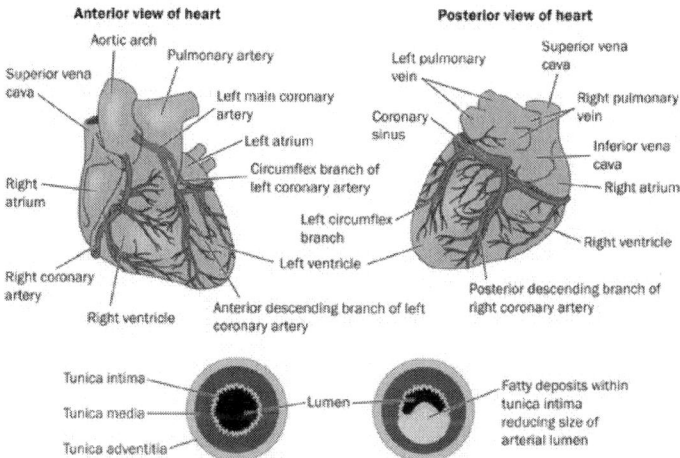

Anterior view of heart

Aortic arch
Pulmonary artery
Superior vena cava
Left main coronary artery
Left atrium
Circumflex branch of left coronary artery
Left circumflex branch
Left ventricle
Right atrium
Right coronary artery
Right ventricle
Anterior descending branch of left coronary artery

Posterior view of heart

Left pulmonary vein
Superior vena cava
Coronary sinus
Right pulmonary vein
Inferior vena cava
Right atrium
Right ventricle
Posterior descending branch of right coronary artery

Tunica intima
Tunica media
Tunica adventitia
Lumen
Fatty deposits within tunica intima reducing size of arterial lumen

Depending on the intensity of pain and the nature of the damage to the heart, pulse and blood pressure may be raised or lowered and the pulse may become irregular. Oxygen saturations may also be decreased if the heart is struggling to pump blood around the body.

Other signs and symptoms can include nausea, vomiting, palpitations, shortness of breath and a feeling of dread. As you can see there is no such thing as a typical heart attack!

The diagnosis is usually made in hospital on the basis of an ECG recording and a blood test to measure changes in cardiac enzymes in the blood.

Management

The management can be broken down into sections dependant on the situation, knowledge and resources available.

From a first aid perspective when emergency services are available once an MI is suspected the patient should be reassured, sat down and given 300mg of aspirin providing they are not allergic to it. Try and keep the patient sitting up to assist with their breathing, but if they are very pale try to raise their legs to improve circulation. If they become unconscious place them in the recovery position.

Talk to the patient and try and get as much information about what happened, their medical history and details of any drugs they take and allergies they have. This will help the Paramedic particularly if the patient becomes unconscious before they arrive.

If help is delayed or not available the next stage involves measures to reduce symptoms and strain on the struggling heart.

If you can measure the patient's oxygen saturation give supplementary oxygen to maintain a saturation level of 95% or above. But do not routinely give oxygen to someone who does not have low oxygen levels (Hypoxia). If the patient also has COPD then saturations can be maintained in the 88%-92% range.

The second drug used is Glyceryl Trinitrate (GTN) this is sprayed under the tongue and causes blood vessels to expand (Bronchodilator) allowing more oxygen through.

The third action is to use a fast acting analgesia the two commonly used are;

Entonox, also called Gas and Air or Laughing Gas.

An intravenous pain killer such as Morphine.

GTN is the primary analgesic in that it directly improves the blood supply. The alternatives relieve pain, but do not fix the underlying problem like GTN.

The use of an anti-sickness (anti-emetic) drug may also be used if the patient is nauseous. Suitable anti-emetic drugs are Metoclopramide, cyclizine or Prochlorperazine.

If you have access to an Advisory defibrillator the patient can be monitored for the first 48 hours and the AED used to treat life threatening rhythms.

The single most useful thing you can do is give aspirin.

Summary

Cardiac chest pain can be a tricky thing to diagnose and many experienced doctors get it wrong from time to time. It is not realistic for the amateur medic to always make a correct diagnosis

Heart failure

Is the inability of the heart to supply the body with sufficient oxygen. It can have many causes;

- Ischemic heart disease
- Enlargement of the heart
- Valve disease
- Diabetes
- High Blood Pressure (Hypertension)
- Obesity
- Smoking
- Drug effects
- Arrhythmias

And can be divided into Left or Right sided heart failure, although both with accompanying symptoms can co-exist.

Left ventricular failure (LVF)

This causes congestion of the veins within the lungs, thus the symptoms shown are manly respiratory despite the problem being cardiac. Symptoms include shortness of breath (dyspnoea) either on exertion or in advanced disease at rest. Patients often need to sleep upright, breathlessness being particularly pronounced when lying flat (orthopnea). This is accompanied by periods of severe breathlessness at night (paroxysmal nocturnal dyspnoea), wheezing, a 'bubbly' chest, dizziness, hypoxia and confusion.

Congestive Cardiac Failure

Right sided heart failure causes congestion of the capillaries in the body resulting in excess fluid leaking into the tissues called peripheral oedema either in the ankles of feet or in the sacral area if the patient is immobile. When fluid returns to the system at night it causes frequent night time urination (Nocturia). Fluid also accumulates in the abdomen (Ascites) and can cause liver enlargement, impairment and jaundice.

Pulmonary Embolism (PE)

A pulmonary embolism is caused by a blood clot lodging in a blood vessel within the lung like a heart attack its effects depends on where the clot occurs, however any pulmonary embolism is a serious condition.

Risk factors for pulmonary embolism include a history of DVTs, use of contraception or long haul flights. Around 0.1% of the population develop DVTs and 10% of people with untreated DVTs develop pulmonary embolisms.

Most cases of pulmonary embolism develop when part, or all, of the blood clot travels in the blood stream from the deep veins in your leg to the lungs.

Symptoms are;

Breathlessness that can come on gradually or suddenly

Sharp pain which can be pin pointed

Pain can increase on inspiration

The patient is often tachycardic and may have coughed up blood

PE's can be fatal.

Angina

Angina is a disease where the coronary arteries have become narrowed due to the build up of cholesterol in the arteries supplying the heart with blood. The patient experiences pain as the heart muscle (myocardium) is starved of oxygen rich blood. There are two types of angina, stable and unstable.

In stable angina the patient generally knows what amount of exercise they can comfortably do without over exerting their heart. They are able to live their life within these boundaries. If they exceed their normal exercise tolerance they experience pain. This is relieved by using GTN spray or tablet which allows more blood to get to the heart muscle.

Treating a casualty that is Bleeding

Types of Bleeding

There are several type of blood vessels in the body, the three well known ones are Capillaries, Veins and Arteries.

Capillaries

These are the smallest vessels and supply a vast network of blood to the skin and organs. If a person is struck and a bruise appears this is actually the result of capillary damage releasing blood under the skin, if you graze your skin then any blood revealed is due to damages capillaries and tends to ooze out. Capillary bleeding is very unlikely to pose a significant bleeding risk however it does open the body up to infection so all grazes etc should be covered.

Veins

Veins are used to take de-oxygenated blood away from the tissues. The blood in them is said to be a darker red as there is less oxygen in it than arterial blood. If a vein is damaged the blood runs out steadily. venous bleeding is life threatening if not treated particularly if internal or in an unconscious casualty that cannot care for themselves.

Arteries

Arteries carry oxygenated blood from the heart to the tissues. Blood from arteries is forced out with each beat of the heart, hence the faster the heart rate the quicker the patient losses blood. Arterial bleeding is the most life-threatening but can be managed using proper techniques.

Dealing with Wounds

A useful acronym for dealing with wounds is PEEP.

(P)osition

Reassure the casualty and get them to sit or lay down depending on the site of injury. This will calm them down, lower their heart rate and thereby lower the amount of blood that may be pumping out of their wound each minute, particularly if the bleeding is arterial.

(E)xpose and Examine

Check the wound for severity of bleeding, contamination and any imbedded or penetrating objects. If there is loose glass, gravel etc on the surface of the wound brush it away. If applying immediate first aid with the intention of contacting health care services soon leave any imbedded objects in place and apply padding to protect them from pressure of subsequent bandaging. Even if your providing definitive care, leave imbedded objects in place until you have gathered your thoughts and equipment to remove them.

(E)levate

If able get the casualty to elevate their own injured limb, this will free you to gather first aid material.

(P)ressure

Apply dressing and direct pressure to wound unless imbedded objects are still in place in which case apply pressure to each side of the object. The use of direct pressure is often underestimated, as even arterial bleeding can be staunched with the application of pressure.

Application of Dressings

Most people would agree it is fairly straightforward applying a dressing to a wound. There are two main ways of covering a wound. You can either; cover it with a pad then apply a bandage or tape on top of the pad to hold it in place or use a readymade dressing consisting of a pad with attached bandage. Readymade dressings come in a variety of sizes depending on type and manufacturer. Standard sizes are;

X-Large Dressing	27.5x20cm
Large Dressing	18x18cm
Medium Dressing	12x12cm
No 1 Ambulance Dressing	12x10cm
No 2 Ambulance Dressing	20x15cm
No 3 Ambulance Dressing	28x20cm
No 4 Ambulance Dressing	32x20cm
Military Field Dressing	10x19cm
Military Field Dressing	20x19cm
Military Field Dressing	30x30cm
Emergency Care NATO	15x17.5cm

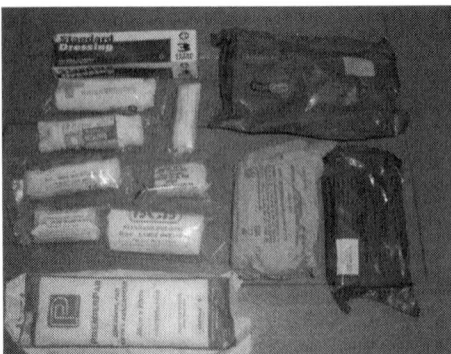

© Chris Breen

A selection of dressings; Civilian on left

Military on right.

Good principals of practice which reduces risk of infection and aid in the control of bleeding are;

Choose a dressing large enough to cover whole wound

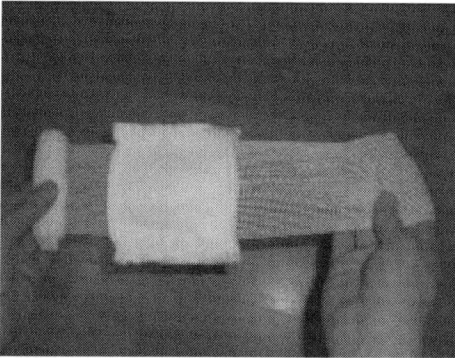

Have casualty hold short end of bandage taut, allowing you to wrap dressing.

Apply bandage to overlap all edges of dressing, tie bandage off on top of wound.

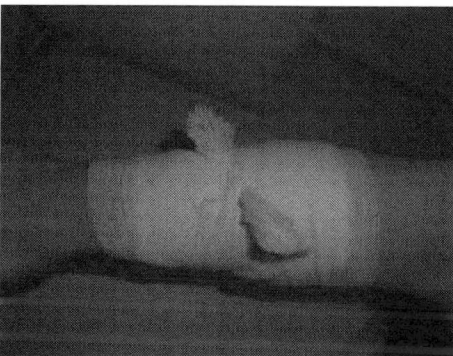

All photos on this page © Caroline Jackson

Bandaging

Cut to Palm off hand

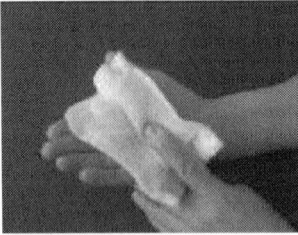

Place sterile dressing over wound.

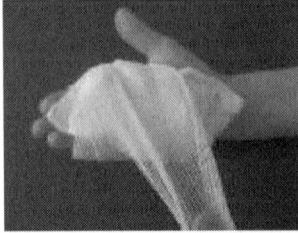

Wrap bandage or second dressing to secure it in place. Start with several turns around hand

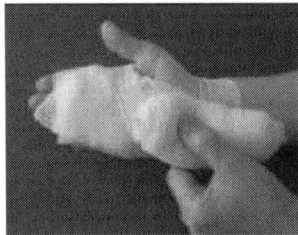

Move down to wrist and wrap bandage around limb.

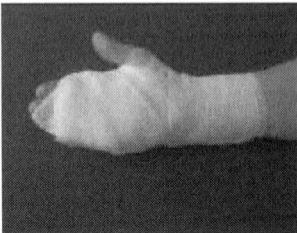

Secure end with tape. Keep thumb and finger ends visible. If they become pale, blue, cramped or numb loosen dressing.
© Caroline Jackson

Slings

There are two varieties of slings commonly in usage;

Broad Arm Sling

This sling is used for support of any arm, hand or shoulder injury. To apply the sling, drape a triangular bandage over the shoulder with the small point under the injured limb and the long end running down the body.

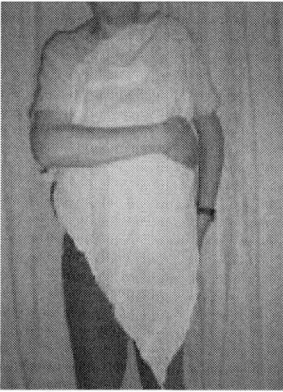

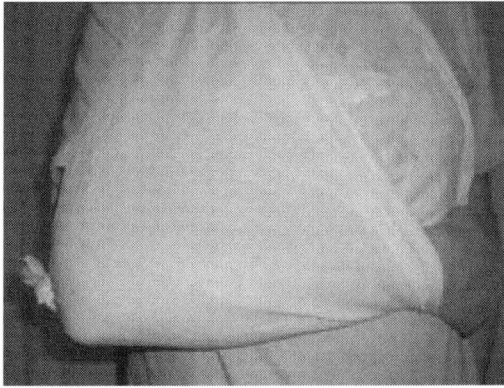

Pick up the hanging end and place over the shoulder on the injured side and tie to the other end from behind. Twist point at elbow and tie single knot to form a pocket which cradles the elbow.

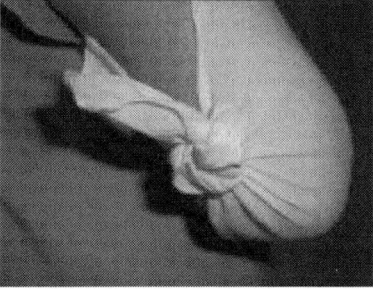

Elevation Sling

This is used primarily to control bleeding in hand and low arm injuries. Have casualty place injured arm across chest pointing upward towards opposite shoulder. Drape triangular bandage over arm with point towards elbow on the injured side.

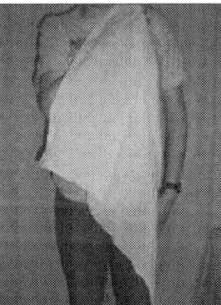

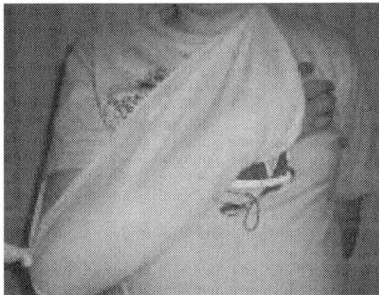

Bring hanging end of bandage under armpit on injured side and tie at back. Twist and tie point at elbow as above.

For both slings ensure fingers are visible to allow circulation checks to be made. If fingers start going pale or blue then dressing/bandages are too tight and need loosening. For added stabilization a broad bandage made from a second folded triangular bandage can be tied across the chest as below.

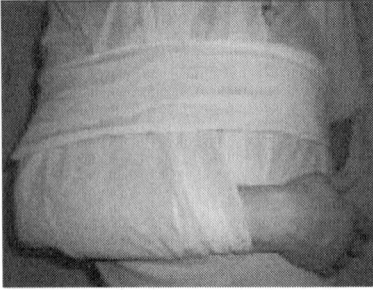

© **Caroline Jackson**

Control of Serious Bleeding

Most bleeding can be controlled by direct pressure and/or elevation. Where it cannot there are a number of options available.

- Indirect Pressure
- Tourniquet
- Packing wounds
- Haemostatic Agents
- Surgical Intervention
- Indirect Pressure

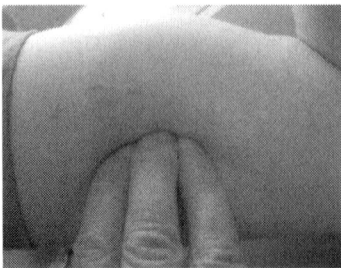

© Caroline Jackson

The two commonly used pressure points are in the arm, see photo left (brachial) and in the groin (femoral). The brachial point is located above the elbow on the inside of the arm in the groove between the biceps and the bone. Applying pressure at this point will slow bleeding giving wounds a chance to clot. The femoral artery is located on the front, centre part of the crease in the groin. It takes a lot of pressure to stop femoral bleeding so your fist or heel to apply pressure.

Treating Traumatic Wounds

Basics

The basics of wound treatment is exactly the same big or small // knife or bullet, there are a number of components which are always the same:

1. Lighting

2. Assessment of injured structures

Nerves / blood vessels / tendons / organs

3. Anaesthesia of the area if possible

4. Exposure

5. Irrigation / cleaning

6. Debridement

7. Primary closure / Delayed primary closure or secondary closure

8. Consideration of the need for antibiotics

Lighting

You need to have good lighting to see what is going on in the wound. It seems whatever position you put yourself in your shadow blocks your light source and the wound appears in shadow. The answer is a good quality head torch – preferably one which has the ability to adjust focal depth.

Assessment

Every wound, same basic process is always the same.

Assess that the structures distal to the wound are working. This is where a knowledge of anatomy becomes vital. You have to know what is normal function looks like and also what structures are in and around the wound.

Tendons

Are any of the tendons cut?

Can all the distal joints work normally?

Nerves

Is sensation intact distal to the wound?

Blood vessels

Are there good pulses?

What is the capillary return?

Wound cleaning

Through cleaning best way to reduce chance of wound infection

Three phases

Cleaning

Irrigation

Debridement

Cleaning: The initial step is the process of removing visible dirt and contamination. Common disinfectants include Povidone, Chlorhexidine, H2O2 or Alcohol (which is very painful in wounds)

In the absence of any disinfectant, water is ok. You should wipe away any visible dirt and contamination in a circular motion from inside out.

Irrigation: The solution to pollution is dilution, large volumes to wash out and dilute any microscopic contaminates in the wound. Normal saline is the first preference, but clean tap water is adequate. Ideally this needs to occur under pressure (7-20 psi) at volumes of 100-1000mls depending on wound

Types of Wounds

Contusion

These are blunt, non penetrating injuries that crush or damage small blood vessels and result in bleeding into the local area. Erythema (or redness) results from the dilation of the capillaries; Ecchymosis (or the bruise itself) results from blood leaking from small blood vessels and losing its oxygen. A hematoma is a palpable lump from where the blood has leaked out of vessels and pools in the tissues. The patient can lose a significant amount of blood before swelling is evident.

There is normally no specific treatment it is just painful and simple analgesia is enough. Usually there is not enough blood loss to be significant from a volume point of view, c\occasional if extensive bruising can be a problem due to blood loss but this is not common.

Large haematoma has the potential to get infected, this presents as increasing pain / fever / swelling. The treatment is antibiotics initially and if not quickly setting may need incision and drainage.

Lacerations

A laceration is a straight cut to the skin, often superficial but may involve deeper structures. The main aim of managing these wounds is to close the skin.

You need to understand that there are many structures you cannot fix or are beyond your experience in a remote clinic environment, but you still need to consider and try and identify what deep structures are injured.

For deep lacerations Providone iodine sprayed into the wound before closing protects against infection. A low-adherent absorbent dressing such as polyurethane foam is ideal with pressure bandaging added if there is much discharge after suturing.

Discharge is usually light and within forty-eight hours, a natural barrier against pathogenic invasion will have been formed and the wound can, if required, safely be exposed at this point. Continued cleaning of such wounds will be unnecessary unless there are signs of breakdown or infection

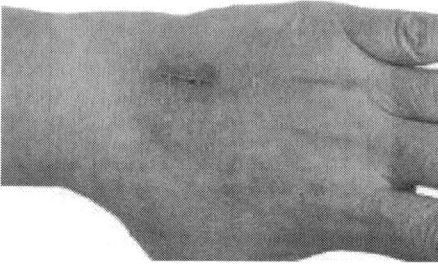

© Birgit Reitz-hofmann - Dreamtime.com

Crush Injuries

When dealing with Crushed fingers and toes you may need to fix an underlying fracture.

Often blood collects under the nail and is very painful, this is easily relieved by heating a paperclip and using it to melt a hole in he nail letting out the blood. If there is loss of a lot of tissue they should be dealt with as open wounds. A low-adherent absorbent dressing such as polyurethane foam or an alginate sheet should be used.

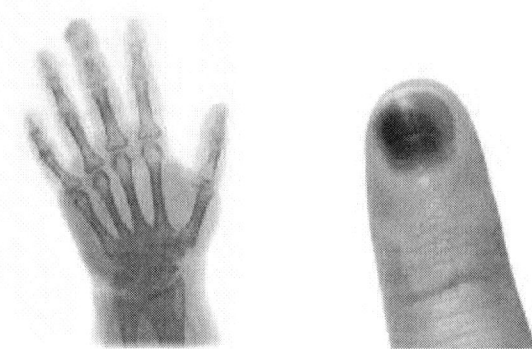

© Tallik Dreamstime.com   © Marcin Pawinski Dreamstime.com

Deep Penetrating Wounds

Penetrating wounds consist of a narrow but deeply penetrating tract; they may contain infection buried deep in the wound. These are caused by knives, low velocity bullets and other penetrating objects. Closing the wound is not an option as it will trap the infection. These wounds need to be opened more under anaesthetic to be cleaned properly. For penetrating injuries involving the trunk see chapters on abdominal and chest injuries. Following cleaning and depending on the size of the hole, either a biodegradable alginate ribbon or a hydrogel with ribbon gauze, loosely packed, are recommended.

Abrasions

Abrasions, although apparently superficial are usually very painful, and commonly have dirt and grit in the wound. They must be thoroughly cleaned and the dressing used must prevent further contamination and absorb discharge. Following thorough cleansing, a semi permeable film dressing can be used for low discharge wounds whilst a polyurethane foam or hydrocolloid sheet is recommended for a wound with high discharge. For high risk wounds use an antiseptic-impregnated dressing.

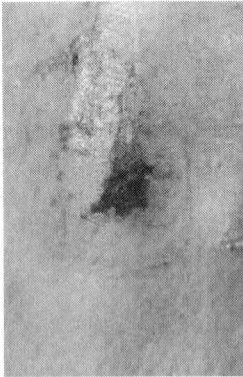

© Szefei| Dreamstime.com

Bites

Bite injuries produce a confined ragged wound with a high risk of infection – that is especially true for human bites. Thorough cleaning is essential. Bite wound should not be closed a short course (5 days) of antibiotics is usually advisable (e.g. Flucloxacillin, Augmentin or Cephradine)

De-gloving Injuries

De-gloving wounds cause layers of tissue to be torn away exposing deep tissues and may cause extensive damage to skin, fat muscle and bone. Such injuries will need thorough cleaning and possible skin grafting.

Nose bleed

Treatment for a nose bleed is to get the patient to sit up and pinch the nose just below the bridge and hold for 10 minutes if it is still bleeding repeat and repeat again. If after 30mins it is still bleeding clear any clots, soak some ribbon gauze in adrenalin and pack into nose. This will apply direct pressure and the adrenalin will encourage the blood vessels to shrink which will help with clotting.

Other methods include simple packing with tampons or gauze or the use of a silver nitrate stick to cauterise the wound (apply for max of 5 seconds). For bleeding in the back of the nasal cavity apply direct pressure to the bleeding point using a balloon catheter which is inflated after pushing it into the nose.

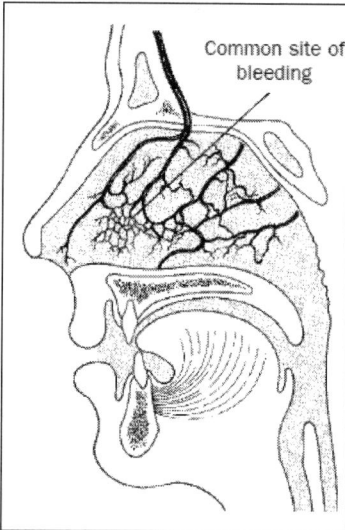

Common site of bleeding

© WHO(2003)P.85

Internal bleeding

In a pre-hospital setting the only effective treatment for internal breathing is rapid evacuation. Supportive treatment for shock is also advised.

Chest injuries and crush syndrome

Chest Injuries and Crush Syndrome

There are several different chest injuries.

Fractures of the chest wall have been previously covered.

Remaining injuries either effect;

- Lungs
- Diaphragm
- Wind Pipe (Trachea)
- Heart
- Major Blood Vessels
- Oesophagus

Lungs

There are a number of lung injuries that can result from trauma;

Pulmonary contusion

Pulmonary contusion is bruising of the lungs causing bleeding. This decreases gaseous exchange and lowers oxygen level in blood. Support patient with oxygen if available.

Pneumothorax (Punctured Lung)

Simple Pneumothorax

A simple Pneumothorax is caused by trauma or can happen spontaneously, tall thin men are more at risk of this. The degree of compromise to breathing depends on size of Pneumothorax. Small tears will heal themselves, monitor in case it becomes a tension Pneumothorax and treat symptomatically.

Open Pneumothorax

An open Pneumothorax is known as a 'sucking chest wound' caused by penetrating trauma which will allow air to enter the chest cavity from outside. Bubbling of blood in the wound may be seen on expiration. Air may be present in the surrounding tissue (Subcutaneous emphysema) which feels like "bubble wrap" when pressed.

This should be covered with a three sided dressing which air cannot easily pass through such as a small plastic sheet or bank card. With three sides taped to the skin it will press firmly against the body when the patient breaths in and will restrict air entering the hole. When they breathe out the chest wall relaxes and air can escape through the side which is not taped.

Tension Pneumothorax

A Tension Pneumothorax occurs when air enters the pleura but cannot escape, as pressure builds up it collapses the lung on the affected side, as it progresses it can also affect the heart and other lung. Potential signs include; diminished or absent breath sound, one sided chest movement, fast breathing, lowering blood pressure, distended neck veins and cyanosis. If you see the trachea has moved away from the midline towards the unaffected side this is a very serious problem. Support blood pressure and oxygenation. The definitive treatment is by needle decompression which can be carried out by a Paramedic or Doctor.

Haemothorax

A haemothorax is bleeding into the chest cavity it will present with both breathing and circulation problems both of which will require support.

Diaphragm

This is a sheet of muscle that stretches across the bottom of the chest and is an essential part of respiration. It can be damaged by blunt or penetrating trauma or by pressure changes during an explosion. If it tears, abdominal organs may become herniated through the tear which will interfere with respiration and may damage the organs leading to loss of function and infection.

Wind Pipe (Trachea)

Damage to the trachea will affect breathing. Monitor respiration rate, oxygen saturation, movement of chest, listen for unequal or absent breath sounds. Give oxygen and suction airway, avoid intubation and positive ventilation with bag, valve and mask unless absolutely necessary as it may further damage the airway. Cover any open wounds, infection is a common problem so prophylactic antibiotics should be given.

Heart

Two conditions affect the heart during trauma;

Myocardial Contusions

Which is bruising of the heart muscle, this shows the same signs as a heart attack and can cause cardiogenic shock it should be treated in the same way with careful monitoring of patient vital signs particularly blood pressure and oxygen saturations. It presents as central chest pain following a history of chest trauma.

Cardiac Tamponade

Which is bleeding inside the sac surrounding the heart. As the blood builds up it compresses the ventricles of the heart and rapidly affects the heart function.. Patients are often also breathless and confused.

Major Blood Vessels

Vessels can be damaged by blunt or penetrating trauma, explosion or deceleration injuries. If the aorta which is the main blood vessel supplying the body is completely severed death is rapid, if it is damaged but not severed a third of casualties die in first 24 hours and half within 48 hours. Aortic dissection is characterised by sudden onset ripping chest pain. Pain is often said to go through to back or into neck or jaw.

Oesophagus

In traumatic injuries the Oesophagus can be damaged by penetrating trauma. The main problem with this is that it allows gastric content to enter the chest cavity which can lead to pneumonia and severe infection.

Abdominal Injuries

The abdomen contains many organs and is separated from the thoracic cavity by the diaphragm. If the injury occurs before inspiration then the diaphragm will be high in the chest, at around nipple level. If the chest is fully expanded then the diaphragm will be flattened. This has to be considered when evaluating injuries. Three types of structure exist in the abdomen;

- Solid Organs
- Hollow Organs
- Vascular Structures

Solid organs include the Liver, Kidney, Pancreas and Spleen these tend to be very vascular and damage causes serious bleeding. Hollow organs such as Intestines, Stomach, Bladder and Gallbladder these rupture when damaged causing their contents to spill into the abdomen, leading to severe infection. The third group of structures include the Aorta, Femoral Artery and Vena Cava, if these are damaged it usually causes life threatening bleeding. If the diaphragm ruptures then abdominal content will enter the thoracic cavity become herniated and interfere with breathing.

Damage to the abdomen may be caused by blunt, penetrating, shearing, deceleration and blast injuries.

If the wound is open then the organs may protrude from the abdomen. Do not try to push them back in, they should be covered with damp dressings or sheets of cling film, do not allow them to dry out.

Crush Injury and Syndrome

A crush injury is compression causing swelling to muscles and / or neurological symptoms whereas Crush Syndrome is caused by a crush injury with systemic effects caused by toxins released from crushed muscles when pressure is released. Approximately half of patients released from prolonged entrapment where crush injuries occur develop acute renal failure and half of those again will require dialysis. Crush syndrome can also cause shifts in blood between different body areas that cause a drop in blood pressure which can in turn lead to reduced level of consciousness.

A related problem is compartment syndrome where the presence of trauma can put pressure on small arterioles stopping blood flow to muscles in a limb. This can be caused by the buildup of pressure due to bleeding or physical forces crushing the vessels. If untreated it can lead to tissue death due to lack of oxygen and as above the toxins released can travel to the rest of the body.

The general rule is if the casualty is trapped for less than 15 minutes release them as quickly as possible if they are trapped for longer than 15 minutes wait for medical help before releasing them.

Manage a casualty with unstable diabetes.

There are currently over 2.8 million people with diabetes in the UK and there may be up to another 750,000 people who have the condition and do not know it. It has now become a standard test if you have contact with medical professionals. Undiagnosed or poorly treated diabetes is a cause of much disability and contributes to early death.

There are two different kinds of diabetes mellitus these are commonly known as type 1 or type 2 diabetes. The type you have determines the body's ability to produce and metabolise the hormone insulin. Insulin is required for the body to make use of sugar in our diet. Most bodily functions rely on fuel in the form of fat and sugar to work. The brain however relies on sugar only.

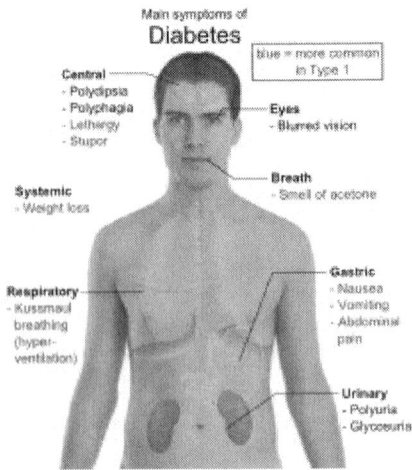

Main symptoms of
Diabetes

blue = more common in Type 1

Central
- Polydipsia
- Polyphagia
- Lethergy
- Stupor

Eyes
- Blurred vision

Breath
- Smell of acetone

Systemic
- Weight loss

Respiratory
- Kusamaul breathing (hyperventilation)

Gastric
- Nausea
- Vomiting
- Abdominal pain

Urinary
- Polyuria
- Glycosuria

© Mikael Haggstrom

Type 1

Type 1 diabetes affects between 5 – 15% of people that have the disease. Type 1 diabetes was formerly called early onset diabetes as it was developed in childhood or before the age of 40. These patents are unable to produce their own insulin. This type of diabetes is therefore controlled with daily subcutaneous insulin injections and regular blood glucose monitoring. These patients learns to vary the amount of insulin they need based on what they eat, their level of activity and blood glucose measurement.

Type 2

Type 2 diabetes usually occurs later in life, when the body can still make some insulin, but not enough, or when the insulin that is produced does not work properly (known as insulin resistance). Triggering factors include obesity, lack of exercise, poor diet, high blood pressure, high cholesterol and genetic disposition. It can develop earlier in life if these risk factors are prevalent. The onset of Type 2 diabetes can be delayed with lifestyle choices, but is incurable once developed and the condition is on the rise. Type 2 diabetes is controlled by diet, exercise, tablets and sometimes insulin.

Treatments

Insulin
Insulin is a hormone which enables cells to absorb glucose from the blood stream which can then be distributed around the body via the circulatory system. Predominantly used to treat type 1, insulin may be prescribed to type 2 patients who are deteriorating or not responding to anti-diabetic meds. If the body is unable to metabolise the sugar it stays in the blood stream, this can damage the vessels and organs it comes in contact with.

Medication

Metformin - this is often the first medicine that is advised for type 2 diabetes. It mainly works by reducing the amount of glucose that your liver releases into the bloodstream.

Gliclazide - increase the amount of insulin produced by your pancreas. They also make your body's cells more sensitive to insulin so that more glucose is taken up from the blood.

Acarbose - this slows down the absorption of carbohydrate from the stomach and digestive tract, preventing a high peak in the blood glucose level after eating a meal.

Nateglinide and Repaglinide stimulate the release of insulin by the pancreas. They are not commonly used but are an option if other medicines do not control your blood glucose levels.

Thiazolidinediones (glitazones) (e.g. pioglitazone, rosiglitazone) - These make the body's cells more sensitive to insulin so that more glucose is taken up from the blood. They are a third line treatment for people who do not respond to other treatments or in whom other treatments are not suitable.

These are the main medications prescribed for type 2.

Glucose monitoring

Only a drop of blood is needed to gain a blood sugar reading. This is usually taken from the end or side of a finger. The normal blood glucose level is between 4 -7 mmol/l before meals, and less than 10 mmol/l two hours after meals, mmol/l means millimoles per litre and is a way of defining the concentration of glucose in the blood.

Measuring Blood Glucose levels

See diabetes in Medical Conditions. Low blood glucose levels are also present in casualties that are starving, intoxicated or exhausted. Low blood glucose known as Hypoglycaemia is potentially a life threatening condition.

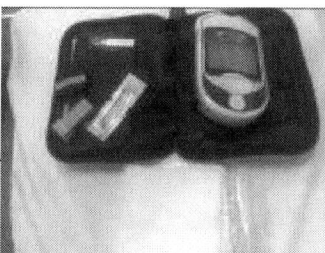

To measure a blood sugar level you will need a Blood Glucose Meter, a test strip and a finger pricker

You need something to prick the finger to obtain a drop of blood. Special safety devices are available but in an emergency a clean, sterile pin or needle will suffice.

Place test strip in meter the display will say "apply blood" or something similar.

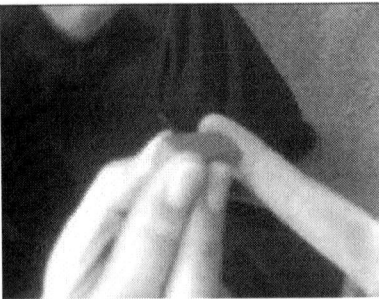

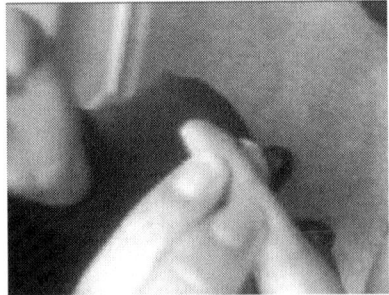

Prick finger, hold finger downwards and apply slight pressure to produce a drop of blood. Stroking the finger with firm pressure will help if blood is not immediately forthcoming.

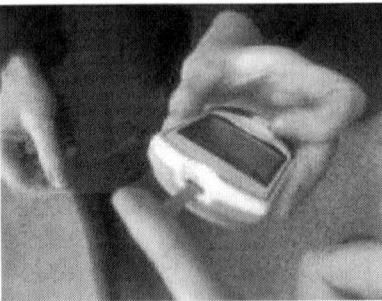

Apply a drop of blood to the top of the strip and wait for the meter to count down, Different models take different amount of time. The model shown takes 20 seconds to analyse the sample.

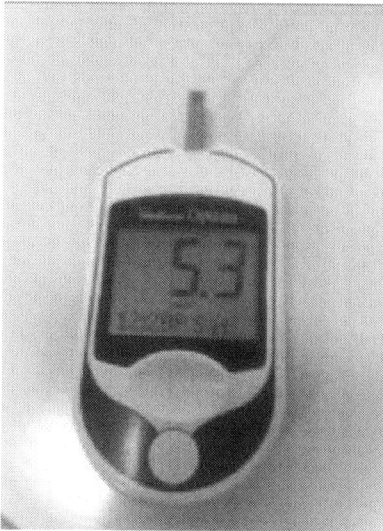

Read and record the blood glucose measurement. If actively treating a patient the level will change quite quickly and can be rechecked ever few minutes.

Symptoms

In both conditions the symptoms are essentially the same. The blood sugar begins to rise (hyperglycaemia) and results in Lethargy, with aching legs being the first indicator.

The next symptom will be increased urine output coupled with extreme thirst. This is because the glucose left sitting in the blood has to be discharged via the kidneys.

After that the patient will rapidly begin to lose weight as the body will have burnt up all of its fat reserves, and become much more lethargic due to the decrease in reserves.

The next stage comes about because the body begins trying to burn protein in the form of muscle-mass as a last-ditch attempt at fuelling itself and the patient will literally waste away, stones lost in days. The by-products of this process are called ketones. If ketones are in the blood they turn acidic and rapidly bring about a condition called ketoacidosis.

The patient's breath may start smelling of ketones which is a 'fruity' or 'pear drops' smell similar to Acetone, however this is a well documented but an unusual symptom.

Emergency Treatment of a patient suffering from Hypoglycaemia 'Hypo'

This is when the blood glucose level falls too low. The actual level at which the patient become symptomatic varies between cases but a reading below 3.5 mmol/l is concerning. A hypo occurs when blood glucose drops to such a point that there is not enough to fuel the brain. This has various causes:

Too much medication

Not enough food eaten

Over exertion

Illness

or a combination of any or all of these.

A patient suffering from a 'Hypo' will gradually become more confused, irritable, aggressive, disorientated and uncooperative. A diabetic 'Hypo' is often confused for intoxication. This can rapidly lead to unconsciousness and seizure, followed by coma and then death.

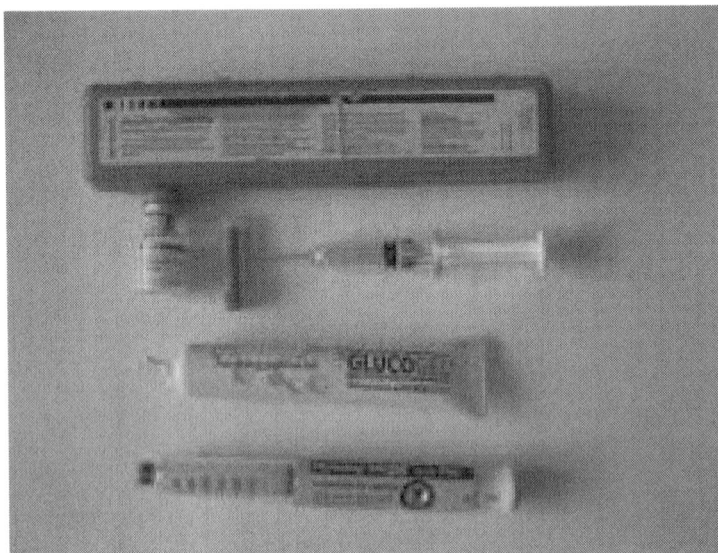

If the casualty is still conscious get them to take sugar in the form of glucose tablets, jam or non-diet drinks. They may have Glucogel (Hypostop) gel which is concentrated sugar.

The information given is for both first aiders and as a suggested treatment for austere situations. In these circumstances gold standard treatment is not always available due to lack of skill, equipment or other resources.

The best practice for the treatment of an unconscious diabetic is to administer bolus doses of intravenous glucose usually 1 or 2 100ml doses of 50% gluscose. The amount that needs to be given is titrated (Calculated) based on the patient's blood sugar, response and level of consciousness.

In order to administer this you would need all the cannulation equipment, a giving set and the glucose which is a prescription only drug (POM). Additionally you would need to know how to take a blood sugar measurement and have the clinical knowledge on how to interpret and act on the results. Further you would need to know how to cannulate safely as injecting glucose incorrectly can cause gangrene which could lead to loss of a limb.

Therefore a glucagon intramuscular injection is a preferred method for teaching to lay people as it is difficult to get wrong and has relatively few side effects compared to IV glucose. It does not involve IV access so has much less risk of introducing infection. Glucagon is also exempt from prescription only (POM) status if administered in an emergency situation so can be done legally by a non HCP. It is taught to carers of diabetics and community first responders for these reasons.

Glucagon releases emergency glucose stored in the body however if the hypoglycaemia was caused by exertion it is likely the patient has already used their stored glucose and the treatment will not work. In this case IV glucose is the only option available

A low tech alternative is to take a substance such as honey or jam and smearing it over the gums of the patient. Care needs to be taken not to cause aspiration but it is ok when there is no alternative.

Managing an Unconsciousness casualty

Unconsciousness as a condition is easy to recognise, the causes may be simple or complex and you may not always be able to recognise or treat them. You can, however ensure survival of the patient or prevent complications by prompt continued care of the airway and correct positioning.

Unconsciousness results from a disturbance in either the brains normal chemical, electrical or oxygen supply.

Two acronyms are useful in remembering possible causes of unconsciousness; FISHSHAPED and BEACHED

- **F**ainting

- **I**nfantile convulsions

- **S**troke

- **H**eart attack

- **S**hock

- **H**ead injury

- **A**naphylaxis

- **P**oisons

- **E**pilepsy

- **D**iabetes

- **B**lood loss

- **E**xtremes of body temp

- **A**sphyxia

- **C**ardiac arrest

- **H**ysteria

- **E**lectrocution

- **D**rug overdose

In order to properly manage an unconscious casualty the following is done.

- Check for Danger
- Check for Catastrophic Bleeding
- Check for Response (AVPU)
- Shout/Call for Help
- Place patient on back

Airway

- Check Airway is Clear; clear if not
- Open the patient's airway by placing one hand on their head to tilt it back and two fingers of the other hand, under their chin to lift the jaw. Consider using a Jaw Thrust If they are likely to have a neck injury. Remember without an Airway, Breathing and circulation will soon cease

Breathing

- Check breathing maximum of 10 seconds, by placing your ear close to the casualty's mouth and looking down the chest. You will be able to see the chest rise, feel breath on your cheek and may hear sounds of breathing.
- If less than two good breathes are heard within 10 seconds start CPR

Circulation

- Check for signs of Circulation such as coughing, opening his eyes, speaking or moving purposefully

Treat life threatening conditions

Perform a Secondary survey – Head to toe

Gain history from bystanders/family

Following treatment of illness or injury place casualty in an appropriate position.

Maintain continuous observation of the airway.

Maintain continuous observation of the level of consciousness (AVPU)

Provide reassurance, talk to your patient in unconsciousness hearing is the last sense to go

Never leave an unconscious patient unattended.

Advanced

Obtain a set of baseline observations if trained to do so.

- Pulse

- Respiration Rate

- Temperature

- Pupil Reactions

- Blood Pressure

- Oxygen Saturations

- Blood sugar levels

Fainting (Syncope) / Vaso vagal attack

Fainting or syncope, is a sudden brief loss of consciousness that may only last a few seconds and is followed by full recovery within a few minutes it is often referred to as a vaso vasal attack.

There are many causes of fainting, including:

- Standing for long periods, such as soldiers on parade

- The sight of needles

- The sight of blood

- Pain

- Emotional events

- Heat

Syncope signs and symptoms

- Dizziness or feeling light headed

- Nausea

- Pale, cool and clammy skin

- Anxious

- Full slow pulse

- Rapid recovery after being laid flat with legs raised

- Loss of conscious

- Collapse

Manage a casualty with a head injury.

Head Injuries

A head injury often causes nothing more than a bruise, lump or headache. There are however several serious conditions which need to be excluded;

Concussion

Concussion is where the brain, which is suspended in Cerebral Spinal Fluid (CSF) shakes within the skull hitting its inside surface, the casualty may briefly lose consciousness and become confused. There may be a brief loss of memory, followed by nausea, dizziness and headache from a few hours to a few days. Recovery is usually complete.

Compression

Compression is usually caused by an injury due to either a skull fracture or laceration to the brain where it has hit the inside of the skull due to sudden deceleration. Compression can be caused by bleeding inside the skull which holds a fixed volume of material or by swelling of brain tissue caused by trauma or infection. Pressure on brain tissue causes patients to display symptoms below as well as increasing disability.

In severe cases the brain can become herniated as it is pushed down into the opening where the spinal column joins the brain. This has the potential to be fatal.

Management

Any patient with a head injury who has a significant mechanism of injury, say from a Road Traffic Collision (RTC), fall or blow also has the potential for a spinal injury.

Assess level of consciousness using the Glasgow coma scale (see appendix 1)

A physical examination of the casualty should be performed. Look for blood with straw coloured fluid from the nose and ear this is cerebral spinal fluid (CSF) and is indicative of a basal skull fracture. Other signs are panda eyes, which are black circles of bruising around one or both eyes and battle sign which is bruising behind the ear.

Check pupil reactions by shining a light directly into the casualties eyes, preferably in dim light. Note the size of each pupil in millimetres, some pen torches have a gauge on the side showing pupils sizes.

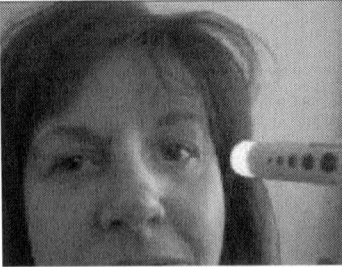

The pupil should go smaller (constrict) in reaction to the light, note if a reaction takes place, if it is brisk or sluggish and if both eyes react the same. A difference in pupil sizes or reaction speed is often a clue to an underlying head injury. Check to see if they can follow the light from side to side and if their vision is blurred.

However do not become fixated with pupils; 10% of the population have asymmetrical pupils (some quite dramatically) and pupil asymmetry is only meaningful if there is other evidence of serious head injury.

Check the casualty can remember what happens (amnesia) a loss of less than a minute is rarely serious. Whereas a loss of greater than 30 minutes usually indicates a serious injury.

Note any history of unconsciousness although not a definite guide less than two minutes is associated with concussion whereas longer periods with compression indicates bleeding or swelling off the brain

Further checks can include;

Hearing in both ears

If they can move all limbs, have normal sensation and no numbness or pins & needles

Finally check to see if they can stand and walk without staggering

Even if the patient passes all the tests they should still be monitored for possible deterioration as initial injury may cause swelling of brain tissue or slow bleeding into the brain. Signs they should be alert for are;

- Increased drowsiness
- Increased headache
- Confusion
- More than one episode of vomiting
- Weakness in Limb
- Facial Droop or Speech difficulties
- Dizziness, loss of balance
- Blurred vision
- Difficulty breathing
- Convulsions or Absences

It is difficult to manage head injuries outside hospital as those with serious head injuries usually are admitted to a Intensive care unit and frequently require surgery.

However management is focused on preventing secondary injury to the brain. You cannot fix the injury that has already occurred, but you can intervene to prevent further damage. Secondary injury has a number of causes the focus is on prevention of hypotension and hypoxia.

Stroke

Stroke (CVA)/TIA

A stroke (Cerebral Vascular Accident (CVA)) is an interference with normal brain function caused either by a clot (85%) or bleeding (15%) causing an interruption to blood flow to the brain. Depending on the severity and location of the damage the patient will exhibit different signs and symptoms. They may lose the use of their arms and legs on one side of the body, or there may be a decrease in strength and power on the affected side or just a heavy feeling in the limbs. Patients can become disorientated and confused, speech may be slurred, absent or they lose the ability to select appropriate words to form sentences (Dysphasia). They may have unequal pupils or develop a facial droop. A headache and high blood pressure often are present..

A Transient Ischemic attack is similar to a stroke, but the symptoms resolve without intervention normally within 24 hours and frequently within minutes or a few hours. Although separate parts of function may return at different times.

A simple way of assessing a patient you think may have had a stroke is through the FAST acronym. It stands for FACE, ARMS, SPEECH, TEST.

FACE

Look for facial droop, dribbling etc

ARMS

Ask them to squeeze both your hands with theirs, feel for a marked difference in strength between body sides. Ask if they can raise their legs and assess in the same way.

SPEECH

Listen for slurring, confusion, using inappropriate words.

Treatment

If administering first aid, the patient should be supported in a comfortable position, where any dribbling can drain away. Administer oxygen in saturations below 95%.

The definitive treatment for CVAs caused by clots is to use a clot busting drug (Thrombolytic). This is only usually given after the patient has had a CT Scan to eliminate a bleed as the cause as giving thrombolytic to someone who has a bleeding in the brain will worsen their condition. It has no role outside hospital.

Managing a casualty that has consumed Poisons

Definition of a Poison

A poison (toxin) is any substance which, when taken into the body in sufficient quantity, may cause temporary or permanent damage either endangering life or seriously impairing body functions. Once in the body poisons attack vital organs, such as the brain, heart, lungs, liver and kidneys. Different poisons attack different organs and produce varying signs and symptoms – they may develop quickly or over a number of days. Although a patient may well recover, permanent damage may occur to internal organs.

Overdose and poisoning is a common complaint we are called to in the Ambulance Service and accounts for 140,000 hospital admissions per year.

Poisons are usually taken in one of following ways:

- Accidentally or Intentionally (self-harm), mal-intent

- or non-accidentally.

A number of factors will affect severity and outcome including age, toxicity of the agent,   quantity and route of exposure.

How Poisons enter the Body

- **Inhalation** – Fumes, gases, solvents, vapours
- **Ingestion** – Liquids, or solids by mouth
- **Injection** – Needles, animal and insect bites
- **Absorption** – Pesticides or herbicides through the skin and eyes

Record

- The event e.g.: when did it happen

- Drug /substance - household product, pharmaceutical / recreational substance, plant / fungi, alcohol, chemicals (CBRN) etc.

- Quantity of the drug/substance ingested

- Collect all suspected drugs/substances

- Mode of poisoning e.g. ingestion, inhalation

- Additional contributory factors – alcohol

- Has any treatment occurred yet?

Poisons are classified as:
- Corrosive / Irritants or

- Non – Corrosive

Corrosive / Irritant Substances
Clinical Signs:
- Lips mouth show signs of corrosion

- Burning / staining

- Severe pain / swelling mouth and throat

- Retching / vomiting

- Abdominal cramps / diarrhoea

- Difficult speech due to swelling of the mucosa

- Odours on breath

Treatment
- Ensure open airway

- O2 therapy (Paraquat with caution only in hypoxic pt's with SpO2 <88% aiming for target saturation of 88-92%)

- Check Pulse

- Never induce vomiting

- Ascertain poison taken / time / quantity

- Nil by mouth unless directed to by container

- Caustics / petroleum dilute i.e. MILK

- Retain samples for Identification

- Transport to hospital Urgently

- Retain vomit for Analysis

- Taking a relative/witness to hospital with the patient if possible

- Ensure open airway

- Administer oxygen

- Assist ventilation if necessary

- CPR with Pocket Mask, Bag / Mask or Mechanical resuscitator (NOT Mouth to Mouth)

- Avoiding Contamination

- Record Blood Glucose level if trained to do so

- Transport in Recovery position

Non – Corrosive Substances

Neurotoxic poisons

Generally affects the nervous system by depressing vital functions; more common ones are:

- Morphine
- Heroin
- Barbiturates

Clinical Signs

- Pinpoint pupils (with opiates)
- Slow and shallow breathing (depressed respiration)
- Lethargy and reduction in activity
- Vomiting and diarrhoea
- Loss of consciousness

Treatment

- Ensuring open airway
- Oxygen therapy in high concentrations

- Assist ventilation if necessary
- CPR if required
- Do not induce vomiting
- Copious amounts of water / milk to dilute and delay absorption
- Place in recovery position and do not induce vomiting, if the patients unconscious
- Keep patient still and quiet to reduce pulse rate
- Do not allow the patient to walk

Poisonous Gases

- Approach the scene with care
- Remove the patient from the poison source
- Ensure open airway
- Administer high concentrations of oxygen
- CPR if required
- Loosen and remove contaminated clothing
- Identify what type of gas was inhaled
- Inform the receiving hospital if possible (pre-alert)
- Transport to hospital

Paraquat Poisoning

In addition to the usual clinical signs, there may be evidence of burning around the mouth.

- Open airway
- O2 therapy only when hypoxaemic to maintain SAO2 @88-92%
- Artificial ventilation only by bag valve mask.
- Do not encourage the patient to vomit

Pesticide and Herbicide Poisoning

- Remove the patient from the source
- Ensure open airway
- Assisted ventilation Bag Mask / Ventilator providing O2
- Encourage vomiting as a matter of priority if swallowed substance
- Remove contaminated clothing taking care not to contaminate yourself
- Wash contaminated skin thoroughly
- If eyes contaminated irrigate with copious amounts of clean water, covering both with soft pad

- Take to hospital for examination (eye causality)
- Take with you, container / sample of the substance / vomit for analysis

Alcohol Poisoning

- Alcohol intoxication is a common emergency & can pose a major problem when combined with drugs in overdose

- When combined with opiate drugs or sedatives, it will further decrease LOC & increase the risk of aspiration of vomit

- Pay particular to airway management & use the recovery position where appropriate

- Always remember to check BM as hypoglycaemia can mimic the signs of alcohol intoxication

- Remember alcohol poisoning can be fatal

Drug Overdoses

Could be accidental or intentional

Management:

- Safety

- DRABCDE – correcting as go along

- Hx – what drug, how much, when taken, how taken, mixed with anything else, collect all suspected drugs to take to A&E, any treatment occurred yet

- Administer high flow O2 if trained to do so.

Some common drugs used in poisoning / overdoses

- Paracetamol

- Aspirin

- Tricyclic antidepressants – amitriptyline, dothiepin

- Heroin and other opiates – morphine, pethidine

- Barbiturates / 'downers' – amytal, seconal

- Amphetamines – speed / ecstasy

- Alcohol

- Organo-phosphates – pesticides, insecticides, nerve agents

- Benzodiazepines – Diazepam, Midazolam

- Recreational drugs – Cocaine, Cannabis

- Beta-blockers – Atenolol, Propanolol

National Poisons Information Service (NPIS)

- NPIS is a service commissioned by the Health Protection Agency that provides expert advice on all aspects of acute and chronic poisoning

- It promotes, supports and develops best practice for the management of cases of poisoning in NHS facilities

- However it does not answer queries from the public but supports NHS Direct (0845 4647) and NHS24 (08454 24 24 24)

- Also available is receiving hospital A&E Dept

- Toxbase (www.toxbase.org Username: AMB101 Password: EMAS) – primary clinical toxicology database of the NPIS & is the first line resource for UK health professionals

Psychological considerations

- May behave irrationally or unpredictably. Remember safety is paramount. Behave sensitively and tactfully with sympathy or gentle firmness where necessary

- Some drugs heighten awareness – limit patients exposure to excessive light & sound?

- Remain objective and professional at all times

- Remain neutral – avoid criticism or judgement – it will not help and may aggravate the situation

Important Points

- Removing contaminated clothing and any contamination of the skin takes priority over everything except immediate life support treatment

- Avoid contamination yourself, particularly hands; always wear protective gloves at this type of incident

- Clear contaminated equipment before use again

- Several of these products produce severe excitable states. Manage patients gently, quietly and with minimum fuss

- Safety first – perform dynamic risk assessment

- Avoid contaminating yourself

- Act quickly, speed is essential

- Ensure open airway

- Assist ventilation if required (never mouth to mouth)

- If unconscious do not induce vomiting

- Conscious (if caustic or petroleum products have been swallowed) give milk, water

- Do not give salt drinks this will induce vomiting

- Save a sample of vomit

- Monitor patient for deterioration

- Keep patient quiet and don't allow them to walk

- Reassurance

- Collect sample of poisons and bottles

Manage a casualty who is convulsing.

Seizures

These can vary in intensity from brief periods of absence where the patient appears to be distracted to prolonged full body convulsions and repeated fits. Many things can cause seizures; epilepsy, CVAs, head and spinal injuries as well as other medical problems. It is believed that 30% of seizures as caused by heart problems when sufficient oxygen is not been delivered to the brain.

Three broad types of Seizures exist;

Absences (Petit Mal)

Tonic Clonic (Grand Mal)

Focal (Jacksonian)

Focal seizures may only affect a single limb and do not necessarily require emergency treatment.

If the patient is known to have seizures and they are generally short in duration (<1 min), let the seizure run its course, protecting the patients head, don't try and restrain them and never put anything in their mouth.

A Tonic Clonic Seizure generally follows four stages;

Indication of Seizure (Aura)

Patient becomes Rigid (Tonic)

Seizure activity (Clonic)

Recovery Phase (Post Ictal)

If the fit is prolonged treatment should be give;

Administer Oxygen if patients oxygen saturations are lowered

Administer Diazepam (Rectal or IV) or Midazolam

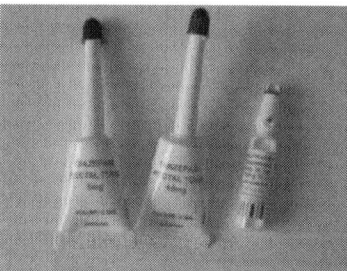

If the seizure is caused by a high temperature "a febrile convulsion" try and cool the patient by; removing clothing, cool sponging and once conscious Paracetamol (Tablet, Liquid, IV or Suppositories) to reduce the temperature. Care should be taken with children not to overcool them and push them towards hypothermia.

If a patient remains in a state of seizure or has multiple seizures for a prolonged period they are at serious risk of sustaining a long term brain injury. Fits lasting over an hour have an 80% chance.

Always check the casualty's blood Glucose measurement and supplement if required, as seizure activity burns lots of energy.

If they have clenched teeth (Trismus) this can compromise the patient airway, consider using a Nasopharyngeal Airway (NPA) and manually supporting the airway.

Febrile Convulsions

A febrile convulsion, also known as a fever fit or febrile seizure, is a convulsion associated with a significant rise in body temperature. They most commonly occur in children between the ages of 6 months to 6 years and are twice as common in boys as in girls

The child is unable to regulate its own body temperature due to an immature hypothalamus in the brain. As body temperature rises rapidly during an episode of infection, usually >39°C most children will experience a brief full body seizure that is tonic-clonic in nature usually lasting 1-2 minutes. But can last up to 15 minutes, a simple febrile convulsion should not reoccur with 24 hours. However a complex febrile convulsion can occur and is characterized by longer duration, recurrence, or focus on only part of the body.

34% of all children between the ages of 3 months and 5 years will have a febrile convulsion and 1:3 risk further convulsions. There is evidence that indicates a higher risk of further seizures if the first seizure occurs before the age of 1 year. However, only 1% of children will go on to develop epilepsy.

Managing Burns

Burns are fourth major cause of trauma related deaths, burns can be classified into three types;

Superficial (First Degree)

Partial thickness (Second Degree)

Full thickness (Third Degree)

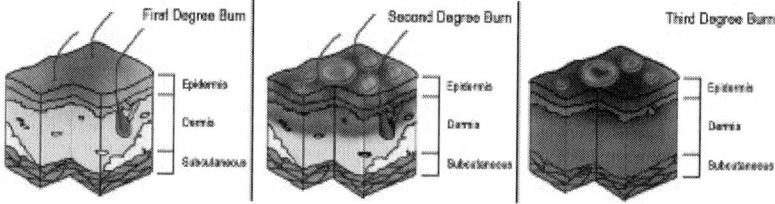

First Degree Burn — Epidermis, Dermis, Subcutaneous

Second Degree Burn — Epidermis, Dermis, Subcutaneous

Third Degree Burn — Epidermis, Dermis, Subcutaneous

© Persian Poet Gal

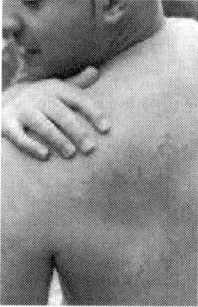

© Arenacreative | Dreamstime.com

Superficial burns only affect the top layer of skin, they are denoted by reddening and swelling of skin and tenderness.

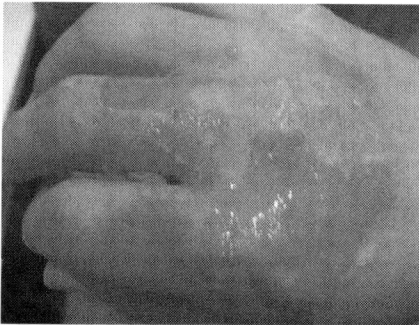

Partial thickness burns affect the epidermis causing reddening and rawness. Blisters are formed from plasma released from tissues. © Alcedema

Full thickness burns affect multiple layers of skin and can affect nerves, blood vessels and underlying muscles.

© Goga312

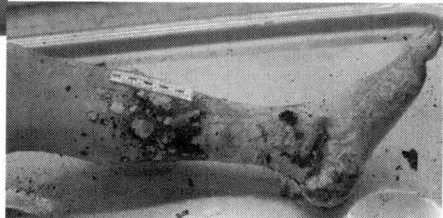

A casualty who is trapped in a burning structure or vehicle can experience a number of problems apart from tissue loss. As always our priority is to **maintain (A)irway, (B)reathing and (C)irculation**.

Burns cause progressive cell death as temperatures rise above 45°C, instantaneously above 60°C, heat is also conducted into surrounding tissues, causing further injuries.

Burns cause fluid loss from cells this may happen over several hours and is relative to the area burned see below.

Injuries of over 15% of the body surface (10% in children) cause sufficient loss of fluid that the patient will require additional fluids to be administered to prevent shock developing.

Early cooling of a burn will reduce the local inflammatory response. Injuries above 25-30% of the body surface cause Systemic Inflammatory Response Syndrome (SIRS). This continues to develop for several hours after the burn.

The clinical signs of SIRS can be delayed. Toxins released from the burn wound further stimulate the SIRS. In the healthy, excessive i.v. fluid administration can be compensated for by an increased urine output. In the burn victim, too much fluid results in excessive oedema.

Smoke Inhalation

This is a serious problem and affects the body in different ways;

Burns to the airway are caused by hot gases from flame, smoke and steam. Usually affecting the upper airway which can swell causing an obstruction. The patient may appear initially ok but as the swelling can occur up to 36 hours later and develops slowly they must be observed carefully. The lining of the airway may become ulcerated leading to secondary infection.

If the gasses are toxic and are deeply inhaled into the lungs they dissolve, leading to chemical injury which can lead to pulmonary failure, this may take hours or days to become apparent.

Absorption of toxic gases through the lungs into the blood leads to blood poisoning.

The two leading causes of death are due to carbon monoxide and cyanide poisoning. Carbon monoxide replaces molecules of oxygen carried in blood it also causes cells to function abnormally.

The patient will experience fatigue, nausea and confusion this can lead to a decrease in brain function and eventually death in severe cases.

It is important therefore to assess their respirations for adequacy and depth. This is a situation where endotracheal intubation is required over a Laryngeal Mask Airway (LMA) or other simple adjunct for the unconscious patient, before the airway closes due to swelling. In all cases the patient will benefit from oxygen and may require assisted ventilation with a Bag valve and mask.

If intubation is not performed early a cricothyrotomy or tracheotomy may be needed to maintain a patent airway. Toxic inhalation may occur from carbon monoxide if petrol, wood or oil was burnt in the fire or from cyanide poisoning if nylon or polyurethane was burned.

Severe industrial Cyanide poisoning is treated with 300ml dicobalt edetate IV followed by 250ml of 10% glucose IV. Premixed antidote kits are available from laboratories that routinely use cyanide.

Burns Treatment

Cooling treatment

Initial management of burns is cooling with clean cold water. Removal of restrictive items, smouldering clothing and application of saline soaked sterile dressings. Commercial dressings such as waterjel are available that contain lignocaine a local analgesia, however they should be used with caution in children as they can quickly lower their body temperatures, these are useful when dealing with superficial or partial thickness burns where nerves are still intact.

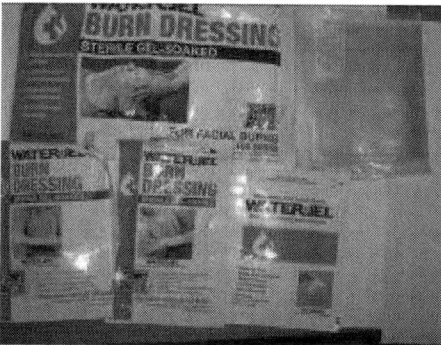

Following initial cooling you need to consider dressings and fluid therapy.

Fluids

A balance needs to be struck between too much and too little fluid – burns less than <30% can usually be managed with oral fluid (ORT is perfect) and titrated to urinating several hundred ml's 2-3 times a day. Burns greater than 30% usually require IV fluids,

All casualties that receive severe burns will benefit from IV fluid therapy to replace lost liquid from plasma. The amount of fluid required is often underestimated, first we need to calculate the body surface area[BSA] that has partial or full thickness burns. This can be done using the Rule of 9s.

Calculating the % burnt

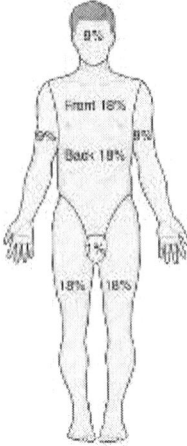

The Rule of 9s.

Head [9%]

Chest and Abdomen [18%]

Back[18%]

Each arm [9%

Each leg [18%]

Genitals[1%]

© Legger| Dreamstime.com

Do not count areas of first degree burn only in estimating the total burnt area for purposes of these calculations.

Initial fluid requirement should be based on 20ml/kg weight of the patient up to 2 litres. Fluid required in the first 24 hours is often underestimated and is based on;

4ml x patient weight in kg x BSA burned.

With half the total being given in the first 8 hours.

Thus a 80kg man with 40% burns would initially need 1.6 litres of fluid, another 4.8 litres in the first 8hrs and a further 6.4 litres in the next 16 hours. For a total of 12.8 litres in the first 24hrs. If the patient is unconscious all of this would need to be given IV.

Significant or critical burns are gauged as full thickness covering 10%+ of BSA or partial thickness of 30%+ of BSA or burns affecting the hands, feet, face, airway or genitalia. Probable mortality is calculated as the patient's age + BSA burnt as a percentage.

Bizarrely one of the killers in burn victims is hypothermia, where blood plasma that seeps into burnt areas is evaporated leading to rapid heat loss and severe hypothermia.

Dressings

Cling film is also very good for dealing with burns it both stops oxygen from reaching the wound, preventing further heat damage and provides a sterile covering. When laying it over the wound place it in sheets rather than wrapping around a limb which if it swells will cause constriction.

For burnt hands sterile burn bags are available, if transit to hospital is delayed these can be filled with flamazine cream. A good natural treatment is tea tree soaked dressings.

Patients will also require some form of fast acting analgesia such as Entonox or IV Tramadol or Morphine. Full thickness burns are often not painful as underlying nerves have been destroyed.

Burn creams and ointments should only be applied to superficial burns that do not require hospital treatment.

Skeletal Injuries

Chapter 6 Fractures

When assessing any casualty with a traumatic injury, some important points should be kept in mind;

Is it a fracture or dislocation?

Does it involve nerves or blood vessels?

Is the patient shocked?

Does it involve any internal organs?

It is important to eliminate potentially life-threatening or complicated injuries before treating as a simple strain or sprain.

When examining the patient always **look** first, then **feel** for deformity before finally **moving** limbs or joints. If your initial observation or tactile examination reveal a significant problem do not the move limb as this will inflict unnecessary discomfort and pain.

When performing an assessment of limbs, remove clothing and evaluate extremities using the pneumonic CSM;

(C)irculation

Is the skin a normal 'Pink' Colour or are extremities pale or cyanosed showing poor circulation. Can pulses be felt away (distal) to the site of the injury. Is capillary refill normal. Do they feel colder than the same limb on the other side.

(S)ensation

Can the casualty feel you touching them? is the sensation the same on both sides and are they able to distinguish between sharp and dull stimulus.

(M)ovement

Can the casualty move limbs, fingers and toes normally in a full range of motion. If pain restricts movement do not force patient to move beyond comfortable limits.

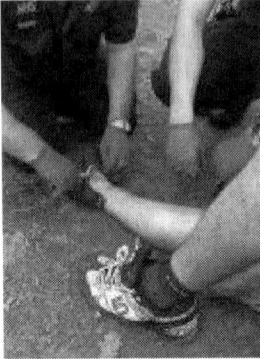

Observe for signs of shock, be aware that multiple injuries may co-exist such as a fracture with dislocation of a joint, internal injuries and/or soft tissue damage.

Referred Pain

In the absence of a clear history of injury the pain the patient feels in a limb or joint, may be 'Referred Pain' this arises when the brain is confused over where the pain stimuli is coming from. E.g. nerves relating to the heart join the spinal cord at T1, T2 level this is the same area that supplies the left arm, which is why people having heart attacks sometimes complain of pain or a heavy sensation in their left arm. A pain in the shoulder with no history of injury result from a more serious underlying problem, such as pneumonia, punctured lung, aneurism, ruptured spleen or ectopic pregnancy. In injury it is also more common in children where hip injuries may present with complaints of knee or ankle pain. In order to accurately identify what is injured always examine the joint and bone above and below the joint where pain is.

Fractures

Some fractures are obvious and involve deformity of a limb or bones coming through the skin, unfortunately most are not. In the absence of x-ray facilities any injury that could be a fracture should be treated as such until proved otherwise.

Fractures are either caused by acute injury, overuse and stress or disease processes such as osteoporosis if there is not a suitable history the injury is unlikely to be a fracture.

If do not know if it is a fracture or not, immobilise it for 72 hours then reassess it – if there is still severe pain and loss of function it makes a fracture much more likely than a sprain or contusion.

Fractures can be diagnosed by any or all of the following;

Pain at the site of injury,

Loss of movement or function,

Swelling or bruising,

Crepitus (grating of bones)

Deformity including shortening, bending or twisting of a limb.

Pain and tenderness caused by fractures appear at the site of injury and around the circumference of the bone. Pain on one side only is more likely to be bruising and a fracture.

Types and sub types of fractures.

Closed Fractures

Closed fractures occur where the bone breaks but is not exposed to the air through a break in the skin. In multiple trauma the skin may be broken but if the fractured bone is nor exposed the fracture is still classed as being closed.

Open Fractures

If the fracture is open part of the bone may protrude through the skin this adds the risk of bleeding and wound infection to that of the fracture. If underlying blood vessels and nerves are affected the fracture is termed complicated.

Stable/Unstable Fractures

One further distinction is that of stable and unstable fracture. Stable fractures occur when the bones are either not completely broken or when the ends are impacted and don't move. Unstable fractures move independently and can cause additional injuries if not splinted securely.

Hairline Fractures

Hairline or stress fractures occur when trauma damages the bone but there is insufficient force to break the bone.

Greenstick Fractures

Occurs in children where the bone splinters on the opposite side of the bone to which the force is applied. This can appear to make the bone bend with obvious deformities.

Simple Fractures

Simple fractures occur when the bone is broken but the two parts remain touching the break can be relatively transverse (less than 30 degrees) at an oblique angle (Greater than 30 degrees) or in a spiral. Without X-Ray it would be difficult to tell them apart other than the fact that transverse fractures tend to heal quicker and are more stable.

Comminuted Fractures

There are many different types of comminuted fractures but most involve the bone fragmenting into multiple pieces. These types of fractures require surgical intervention to repair and involve the use of screws and plates to rebuild shattered bones, some may also require external fixation.

Avulsion fractures

Produced by muscle contraction or stretching of ligaments. These cause pieces of bone to break off where the muscle connects to the bone.

Displacement of fractures

If the bones have moved away from their normal positioning then the fracture is said to be displaced and unless it is repositioned it will either heal with a deformity or not heal at all.

There are different types of displacement which can exist on their own or in combination.

Lateral – Displaced to side of other part of bone

Posterior - Displaced behind other part of bone

Angled - Displaced at angle to other part of bone

Rotated - Displaced at rotation to other part of bone

Management

When dealing with any fracture where urgent evacuation is not possible realign the bones to the closest normal anatomical position you can achieve then splint them. If the bones are then forced to heal in this position the amount of function that returns will be dependent on the accuracy of the realignment.

Support hand, arm and shoulder injuries against the body with slings or straps as appropriate. Lower limbs should be elevated when the patient is lying down. Give analgesia appropriate in strength to the injury.

How Bone Heal

Damaged bones can replace themselves completely given time. When a bone is fractured a blood clot forms at the site of the injury. The body then sends all the materials needed for bone replacement to the injury site and this replaces the clot. In well aligned bones a soft callus joins the bone fragments together and stabilises them. If the bone fragments are not aligned or separated union of the pieces can still take place but the join is often distorted and prone to further damage. This bridging phase takes 3 to 4 weeks. Over the next few months consolidation occurs and the soft callus is replaced by a hard bony callus although it may take up to 2 years before the bone remodels itself to its original shape.

Blood Loss with Fractures

The most serious fractures are those of 'Long Bones' damage to these bones can produce massive blood loss. Blood is lost through three mechanisms;

Damage to large blood vessels

Leakage from Bone Marrow

Bleeding from muscles

The average adult has 5-6 litres of blood in their bodies, a more accurate measure is;

70ml/Kg Adult

80ml/Kg Child

100ml/Kg Infant

Typical long bone injuries have the following blood losses;

Humerus 500ml-750ml

Tibia 500ml-1000ml

Femur 1000ml-2000ml

Closed Pelvic Fracture 2000ml-3000ml

Open Book Pelvic Fracture 4000ml

A 40% Blood loss is classed to be Life Threatening. If you have a normal total volume of 5000ml (5L) 40% is only 2000ml (2L) which can easily be lost in Long bone fractures.

Treating Fractures

There are two main aims in the treatment of fractures. To ensure ends of bones at point of fracture meet without deformity and to restore full function of the affected part.

The first step in treating any fracture is to determine if the bone has been displaced this can be determined by careful examination of the affected area and comparison to the opposite side of the body. A shortened limb on affected side would suggest a lateral or posterior dislocation. A limb moving in an unnatural way could indicate an angular displacement. A hand or foot pointing in the wrong direction suggests a rotational displacement.

SAM Splint

A flexible splint such as a SAM Splint, can be moulded to support a variety of fractures for both short term use and where plaster is not available.

© Caroline Jackson

Fingers and Toes

Any fingers or toes that are fractured should be padded and strapped to the neighbouring digit. They should take 3-6 weeks to heal.

Hands

Fractures to the bones of the hand should be padded and bandaged, if the injury is at or near the wrist, splinting should include the forearm to maintain stability. Fractures to the hand and or wrist can take 4-12 weeks to heal dependant on location and complexity. A flexible splint can be moulded as an improvised back slab then bandaged into place.

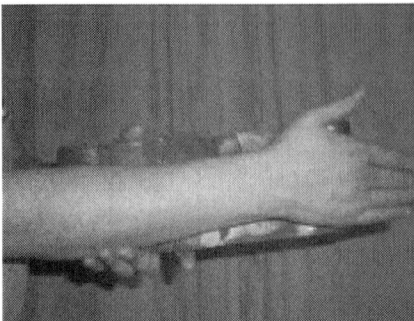

Feet

Fractures of the bones in the feet are difficult to confirm, adequate support can usually be achieved with a boot but the foot should be monitored in case excess swelling effects blood supply. If the damage is to the heel then it is unlikely they will be able to walk on it, foot injuries should take between 3-12 weeks to heal dependant on location and complexity.

Ankle

It is sometimes difficult to distinguish between sprains and ankle fractures. If pain persists for more than a few days and the patient is unable to weight bear treat as a fracture unless proved otherwise. If any deformity is present realign before splinting. A flexible splint bent into a 'U' shape and secured to the lower leg will provide support. If the fracture is minor the patient may be able to still walk on it once splinted. It should take around 6 weeks to heal

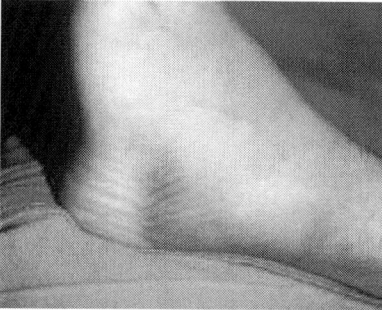

Most ankle injuries are ligamentous sprains.

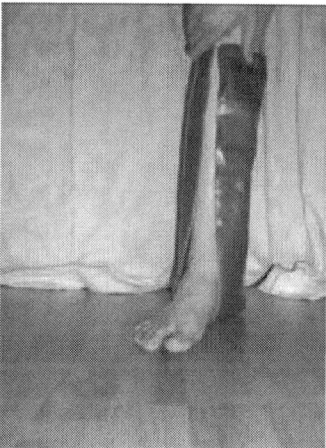

Ottawa Rules for Fractures of the Ankle

The presence of a fracture is more likely in patients with any pain in the area around the bones that protrude either side of the ankle (malleolus) and 6cm up the fibular (malleolar zone) and the inability to walk four weight bearing steps immediately after the accident and upon later examination.

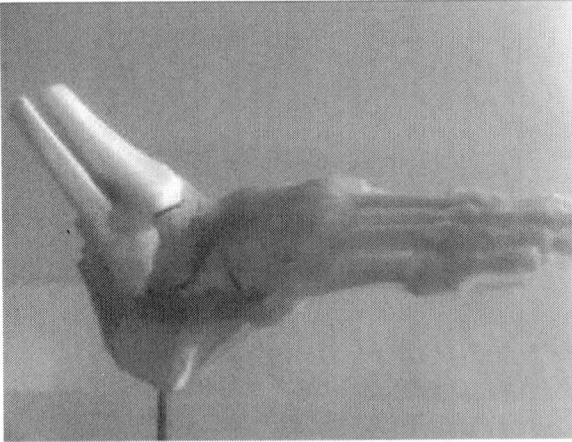

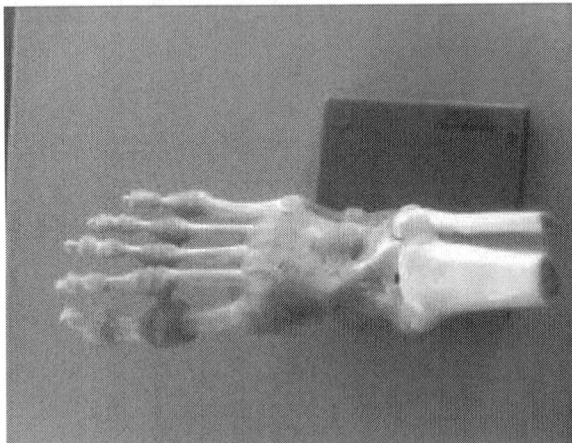

Ottawa Rules for Fractures of the Foot

The presence of a fracture is more likely in patients with foot injuries with any pain in the top of the foot (mid foot zone) and any of the following:

Tenderness at Navicular bone just below the malleolus (see above).

Tenderness at base of the little toe (5th metatarsal) remembering the bones of the toes extend much further back into the foot than the portion where they divide and articulate.

Inability to walk four weight bearing steps immediately after the accident and in upon later examination

Ottawa Rules for Fractures of the knee

The presence of a fracture is more likely in patients with knee injuries with any of the following:

Over 55 years of age

Tenderness at the head of the fibula

isolated tenderness of the kneecap

inability to bend knee to 90 degrees

inability to walk four weight bearing steps immediately after the accident and upon later examination

Forearm (Radius/Ulna)

Any fracture of the forearm is going to affect the wrist and both need to be immobilized together. Once splinted the injury can be further protected by placing in a low arm sling with a broad bandage holding it against the body. It should take around 6 weeks to heal.

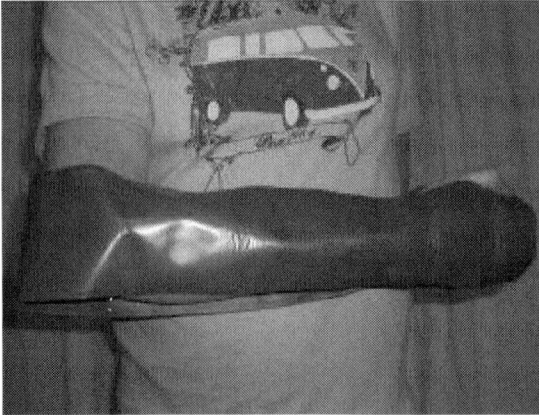

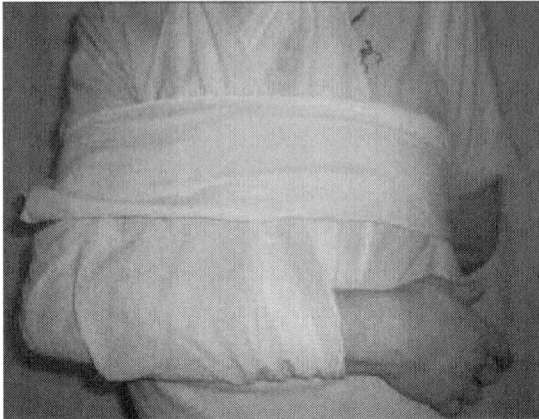

Elbow, Upper Arm (Humerus)

To immobilise the elbow or upper arm use flexible splint, sling and broad bandage as Forearm above. Should take around 4-10 weeks to heal

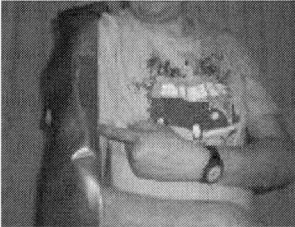

© **Caroline Jackson**

Shoulder Blade (Scapular)

To immobilise the shoulder use a sling and wide bandage as for the Forearm above it should take around 4-6 weeks to heal

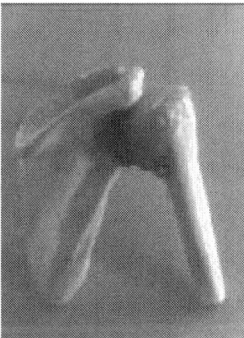

Collar Bone (Clavicle)

To immobilise Collar Bone (Clavicle) use sling and wide bandage as above. It Should take around 3-8 weeks to heal.

Knee and Lower Leg (Tibia, Fibula)

Lower leg fractures need to be immobilized by placing splints on either side of the lower leg. Any fractures of the knee require the ankle to be immobilized as well. Lower leg injuries will take around 10-24 weeks to heal.

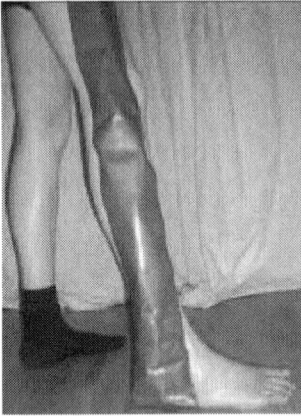

© **Caroline Jackson**

Kneecap

A fracture of the kneecap will need immobilization from ankle to hip with a straight splint at the back of the leg it should take around 4-6 weeks to heal.

Upper Leg (Femur)

A lot of force is needed to fracture the femur, and femoral fractures are often associated with other serious complications. The strong muscles in your thigh will cause fractured bone ends to overlap and damage surrounding tissue and blood vessels leading to serious bleeding. A femoral fracture can be identified by;

Shortening of the limb

Swelling

Pain

Signs of shock

If the femoral artery is damaged death from internal bleeding can be rapid. In order to minimize bleeding traction should be applied. But this is contra-indicated if there is damage to either;

Pelvis

Knee

Top of Femur

There are a number of commercial traction splints available such as the Kendrick, Sager, Hare and Donway Splints. All of which cost around £100-£900.

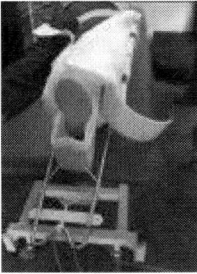

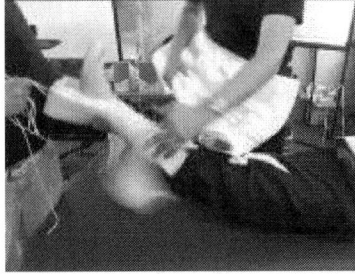

All of the splints work in a similar way and if a dedicated splint is not available one can be improvised using Ski or walking poles, wooden staves etc

The splint provides a fixed point at the hip, additional points down a ridged frame to support the leg and an anchor point beyond the heel from which traction can be applied to a strap around the ankle. If the splint needs to be left on for any time the knee needs should be slightly flexed to avoid damage. The ankle needs to be padded to prevent damage to the circulation of the foot.

Hip

Damage to the ball or socket of the hip joint is very painful and usually requires surgical repair. It is often diagnosed by an obvious shortening of the effected limb and an external rotation of the foot.

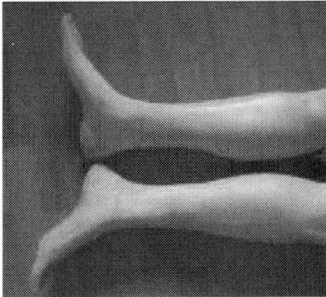

Pelvis

Fractured pelvis should be suspected with any high velocity injury such as falls or RTCs. If the pelvis is entirely broken the patient feet will both be externally rotated this is known as an Anterior-posterior or open book fracture. The main complication of a pelvic fracture is major blood loss as mentioned above there are major blood vessels passing through the pelvis to supply circulation to the lower extremities. Other problems can occur if splinters of bone penetrate abdominal organs. Stable fractures should take around 4-6 weeks to heal. The pelvis can be stabilized by a wide belt such as used for climbing or a purpose made pelvic splint as below.

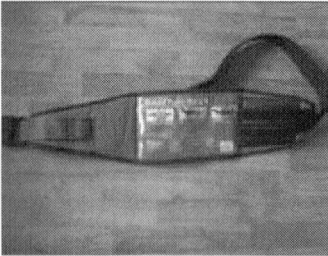

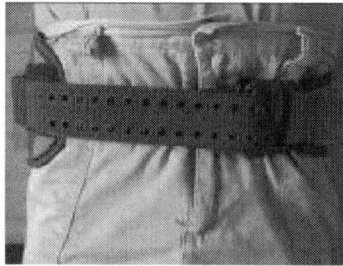

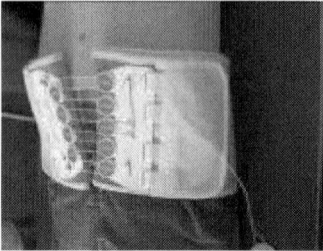

Pelvic splints should be applied to any casualty where there is a suspicion of Pelvic trauma or where they have been involved in an incident of blunt trauma which may impact the pelvic region and have a systolic blood pressure of <110

Due to the forces needed to fracture a Pelvis the patient often has other serious injuries.

50% Serious Head Injury

50% Long Bone Fracture

20% Serious Chest Injury

There are different types of Pelvic Fractures;

60-70% Lateral Fractures

15-20% Open Book Fractures

5-15% Vertical Fractures

The most common type is a Lateral Fracture mostly caused by side impacts these rarely require operation and heal with bed rest. The other two share a 6% mortality rate and are often associated with severe bleeding.

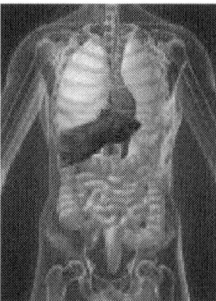

Ribs

© Sebastian Kaulitzki | Dreamstime.com

Fractures to the ribs themselves usually heal without further intervention and should take around 4 weeks. The only real issue is pain and complications from not coughing or deep breathing because of the pain (infection). The only treatment normally needed for simple rib fractures is pain killers such as a non-steroidal anti-inflammatory such as ibuprofen. Strapping of the chest is no longer recommended.

Fractures to ribs can interfere in ventilation of the chest. If multiple adjacent ribs are broken in more than one place a 'flail segment' is created. The segment moves independently from the rest of the chest wall causing pain and impeding respiration. Pieces of ribs can penetrate the lungs causing a heamothorax (Blood in the pleural cavity) or a pneumothorax (Air in the pleural cavity). See section on chest injuries for more details.

Managing Dislocations

When force is applied to a joint the first thing to occur is a mild sprain and the ligaments are strained, as progressively more force is applied a severe strain occurs and if the force continues the joint will dislocates.

Jaw
Jaw dislocation is the displacement of the jaw from the rest of the skull, dislocations can be caused by traumatic and non-traumatic means. The jaw can dislocate in any direction, but moving forward dislocations are the most common, backward dislocations can be caused by a direct blow.

Patients have pain and are unable to open or close mouth, you should check for damage to the mouth and the stability of the jaw for fractures. Other symptoms include a misaligned bite, difficulty speaking, dribbling, jaw may be sticking out.

Shoulder
Shoulders are the most common joint that becomes dislocated and the easiest to rectify.

When examining the patient the normal round symmetry of the injured shoulder looks squared off, they will hold arm in the most comfortable position and resist any attempts to move it due to pain. Check for underlying fractures and ensure the patient still has circulation and sensation along the affected arm..

Elbow
The elbow is a sturdy joint and takes a considerable force to dislocate. Due to this a significant amount of elbow dislocations also have associated fractures. The elbow can be displaces to the front or more often the back.

Finger

Each finger has two joints with a third where it joins the hand, the most common dislocation is to the middle of the three which is the nearer joint to the body of the hand. It can dislocate to the front, back or side with the patient having reduced control over it.

Hip

Hip dislocations can be to the back commonly caused by impacts in road accidents, to the front caused by falls or to the side usually associated with a fracture.

In all dislocations the patient is in severe pain, has severely limited movement in the limb. There is also a possibility of nerve or blood vessel damage. Damage to the femoral artery can cause fatal internal bleeding.

If it is a dislocation to the back the leg will be internally rotated towards the centre of the body whereas in a front dislocation the leg is externally rotated. In patients with total hip joint replacement dislocations are not uncommon but not usually associated with significant injuries in the same way traumatic dislocations are.

Knee

Knee dislocations are usually accompanied by extensive soft tissue damage.

Kneecap

When dislocated the kneecap usually moves to the outside and the deformity is obvious when compared with the other leg. The patient will keep their knee flexed in the most comfortable position.

Sprains & Strains

Sprain

A sprain is an injury to ligaments which are strong tissues which support joints and attach bones together. They can be injured, by being stretched during a sudden pull.

Strain

A strain is stretching or tearing of muscle fibres. Caused by muscle stretching or sudden contraction such as with a seizure.

Treatment

For a long time in First aid Strains and sprains were treated using treatment based on the RICE acronym. Later we moved on to a two phase treatment of RICE followed by MICE where after the initial period the injury was mobilised instead of Rested. Now we have PRICE and HARM.

Protection	**Heat**
Rest	**Alcohol**
Ice	**Running**
Compression	**Massage**

PRICE

Protect

Protect the injury from further damage.

Rest

Rest the affected joint or muscle for 48–72 hours following injury. Keep weight off lower limb injuries

Ice

Ice works on muscle strains and sprains, particularly in the first 48-72 hours following the injury. Ice reduces swelling and provides some pain relief by numbing surrounding tissue. Cooling encourages warm blood to the injury site, bringing oxygen and nutrients to aid in the healing process. Never apply ice directly to the skin and only apply for between 10 and 30 minutes for a time. Cooling can be achieved with a chemical ice pack or a bag of ice wrapped in a towel.

Ice shouldn't be applied to any casualty that has peripheral vascular disease, raynauds syndrome or sickle cell anaemia.

Compression

Compress using tubular gauze or plain gauze bandage for first 48-72hrs, ensure that the bandage supports the injury without affecting blood flow. After this time it is best to mobilise the joint but gauze can still be applied to weight bearing joints for additional support.

Compression is applied to prevent swelling and should be applied first thing in morning after waking up, it has no effect on existing swelling. Do not use it at night or when the limb is elevated.

Recent research had cast doubt over the effectiveness of compressing injuries with double layered tubular gauze, as the calf is bigger than the ankle therefore uniform compression cannot be maintained equally along a limb. Most emergency departments no longer advocate the use of supporting bandages however if one is needed a crepe bandage would give better compression.

Elevation

Elevation is intended to reduce swelling, for lower limbs support on a stool at hip level or in bed on a pillow. Keep arms in an elevation sling. Once the swelling has stopped you no longer need to elevate the limb. HARM For the first 72 hours avoid the following; Heat Avoid heat initially as it discourages blood flow, after the first 72 hours the inflammation should have subsided and heat therapy may be soothing.

Alcohol

Alcohol causes blood vessels to get bigger (vasodilatation) which increase sub dermal bleeding (bruising).

Running

Running or any other form of impact exercise will cause more damage.

Massage

Massage will also increase bleeding and swelling. But after first 72 hours, gentle massage may be soothing.

Eye injuries

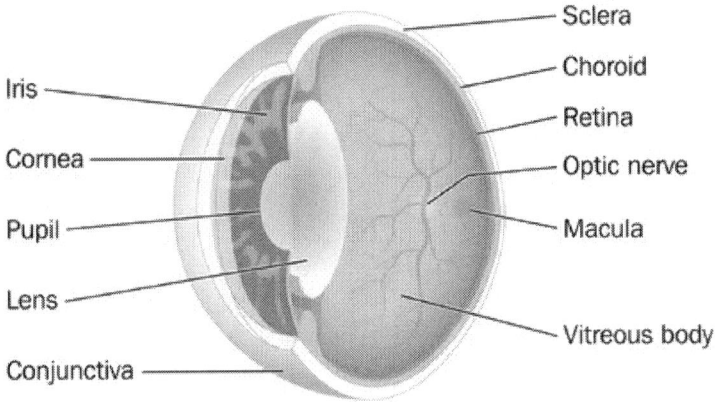

© Legger/ Dreamstime.com

The eye is easily damaged but usually heals well from small eye injuries.

Foreign Objects

Grit can be blown into the eye and either sticks to the cornea causing irritation and/or damage to the surface of the eye.

Trauma

A flow to the face can damage the soft tissue around the eye causing inflammation; which can affect vision and may cause blindness in the affected eye.

Occupational accidents from drilling, grinding can cause small pieces of metal to become embedded in the cornea these near treatment in a hospital or minor injury unit.

Welding activity can cause flash burns, chemical splashes can get in eyes causing damage

In a workplace where welding is undertaken a painful flash injury may occur unless personal protective equipment is used correctly.

A chemical splash in the eye can cause permanent loss of vision and needs prompt first aid and medical care.

Symptoms and signs

- Pain in, or behind, the eye

- Spasm of the eyelids

- A continuous flow of tears from one eye

- Reduced or altered vision, or even loss of sight

- Blood visible in the eye, or bleeding around the eye

Chemical Burns

- Reassure Patient

- Flush the eye with saline or water unless chemical hazard sheet warn against it.

- Advice the patient not too move either their eyes if possible.

- Once the chemical has been flushed from the eye, cover the injured eye with a clean eye pad or wound dressing.

Small Foreign Body

- Tell the patient not to rub the eye.

- If the foreign body is visible on the white part of the eye, ask the patient to blink several times causing tears to try to remove it. If this doesn't work seek further medical advise as it may cause scratches and scarring may occur.

- If the foreign body is on the coloured part of the eye, do not try to remove it.

Flushing

Pour the fluid from the nose end of the eye toward the outer corner to avoid accidentally contaminating the uninjured eye. Tilt head to injured side to aid flushing water away.

Embedded Large Foreign Body

If there is a large foreign body in the eye, do not attempt to remove it, but pad around the eye socket to avoid pressure.

Other injuries

- Check the patient for any other injuries, particularly if a blow or fall was involved.

- Check the level of consciousness and ensure that the airway is clear.

- An injury around the eye may be associated with a head injury.

Welder's flash

Excessive glare (or bright light from a welder) can damage eyes. The patient may complain of severe pain in the eye(s), with a 'gritty' feeling. The eye may be sensitive to light and may be watery and/or red.

Treat by bathing he affected eye and seeking further medical help.

Additional Skills

Measure respiration.

The assessment of breathing includes providing oxygen and ventilation support if required do not move beyond the breathing stage until this if required is provided.

Once an airway is established; look down the body. If the windpipe is completely blocked but the casualty is still making a respiratory effort then you may still feel and see chest movements, so the presence of breath must be verified. If the blockage is in one of the branches of the windpipe leading into the lungs then chest movement may be uneven.

Observe for a maximum of 10 seconds, in that period you should see and or feel at least two breaths. If breathing is inadequate CPR must be started. This can be achieved by mouth-to-mouth ventilation with or without an airway adjunct or with a bag, valve, mask device (BVM)

RESPIRATION RATE

Is the breathing:

Normal

Normal breathing is regular, un-laboured, quiet and off moderate depth.

Deep

Excessively deep breathing

Shallow

Very small breaths

Laboured

Indicators of laboured breathing are; the patient is leaning forward with hand on knees (tripod Position), nasal flaring, inward movement of the muscles between and below the ribs as a result of reduced pressure in the chest (retractions), using the shoulder, neck and other muscles (accessory muscles) to expand the chest cavity and allow more airflow.

Normal respiration for Adults is *12 - 20 breaths/minute*

Abnormal 10-12 and 20-30 at rest

Serious <10 or >30

Normal Child range varies with age:

30-40 Resps/min newborn – 1 year Old

20-30 Resps/min 2 – 4 years Old

15-20 Resps/min 6 – 12 years Old

12-16 Resps/min at 14 Years Old

Remember: An increased respiration of an injured patient at rest may be the first sign of developing shock.

Manage a casualty with spinal injury

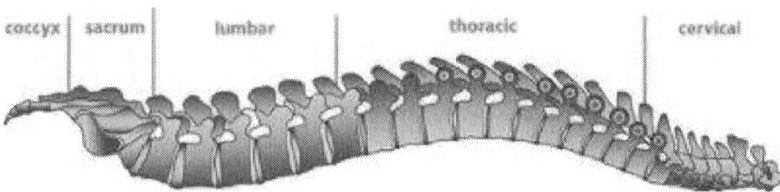

© Maryna Melnyx| Dreamstime.com

The spine is divided into five sections the cervical, thoracic, lumbar, sacrum and coccyx. Most spinal injuries occur in the cervical spine. Mainly as stresses are placed upon it as the head is shaken due to sudden acceleration or deceleration forces. These may be applied during traumatic injuries such as RTCs, blows and falls from heights.

The cervical spine is made up of seven cervical vertebrae separated by inter-vertebral disks and joined by ligaments. They are referred to as C1 to C7 starting from the base of the skull through to the top of the thoracic spine. Damage to C1 or C2 is often fatal if the spine is compromised as the nerves joining the spine at this level control breathing.

A set of rules to eliminate serious injuries to the C Spine is called 'clearing the C Spine' If the following apply

Fully alert (GCS 15) see Appendix 1

Not intoxicated

No distracting painful injury

No neurological signs or symptoms such as 'tingling'

No tenderness in the midline of the neck

And if any of the following are relevant;

Neck pain is present but has a delayed onset

Has walked unaided since injury

Neck injury followed a rear end shunt

If the spine has been 'cleared' then immobilisation may not be necessary. However poor spinal management can have devastating effect on a casualties life and recovery if in any doubt about the presence of a spinal injury immobilise the casualty particularly in the following circumstances.

Fallen >1m

Diving accidents

RTC>60mph

In rollover RTCs or ejected from vehicle

Pedestrian or Motorcyclist in RTC

Patient over 65

Any casualty that is unconscious or has a head injury should be considered to have a cervical spinal injury until proven otherwise. These casualties should be immobilized.

The first step is manual immobilisation and involves holding the patients neck in a neutral position.

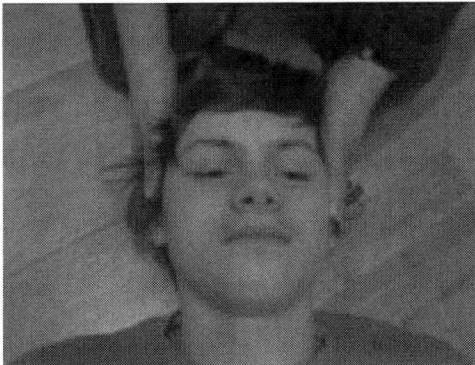

© **Caroline Jackson**

Manage the use of ligature removing devices.

Despite every effort to ensure the safety of members of the public and detainees there is always a risk that they will attempt to self-ligate. This can occur either by securing a ligature around the neck and suspending it from a ligature point, or by tightening it around the neck to cut off the airway. All staff working in areas where ligature cutters are provided will be instructed in their use.

Staff must retain the cut ligature for later inspection. In the event of injury to the patient, or fatality the ligature will form part of the investigation. Where part of the ligature remains attached to a ligature point, it should not be removed until this has been authorised. Where possible, staff must avoid cutting the knot, as this may be required for forensic investigation and will be harder to cut through due to having multiple layers of material.

If there are any injuries relating to the cutter being used, these must be recorded.

Staff should always ensure their safety before attending an injured person. Staff should ascertain whether the ligature itself may present a risk e.g. pressurised lines and live electrical cables may be used to hinder rescue.

A ligature cutter is most effective when used to cut softer and thinner materials e.g. Shoe laces, string, linen, headphone cables and similar. The ligature cutter will cut tougher materials e.g. leather, towelling, some steel cables, electrical flexes, but more effort may be required and the cutting process may take longer.

Using the ligature cutter,
The rounded and blunt end should be initially placed flat against the person's body so that it can lid under the ligature. Where possible, it is recommended to try and cut to the side of the neck. The natural soft tissues and hollows may ease the insertion of the cutter blade. This will also reduce any pulling onto the airway upon cutting (as would occur if the cutter is inserted at the back) and reduce likelihood of causing further trauma to the airway, as may occur if inserting from the front.

Once the ligature cutter has been located between the person's body and the ligature, the ligature cutter should be turned so that the sharp edge of blade faces the ligature i.e. with the opening away from the person. At this point staff should pull away from the person's body, using a rocking or sawing motion, so that the ligature cutter cuts through the ligature material.

Picture from Northampton Healthcare (2013) Procedure for the safe use of Ligature Cutters.

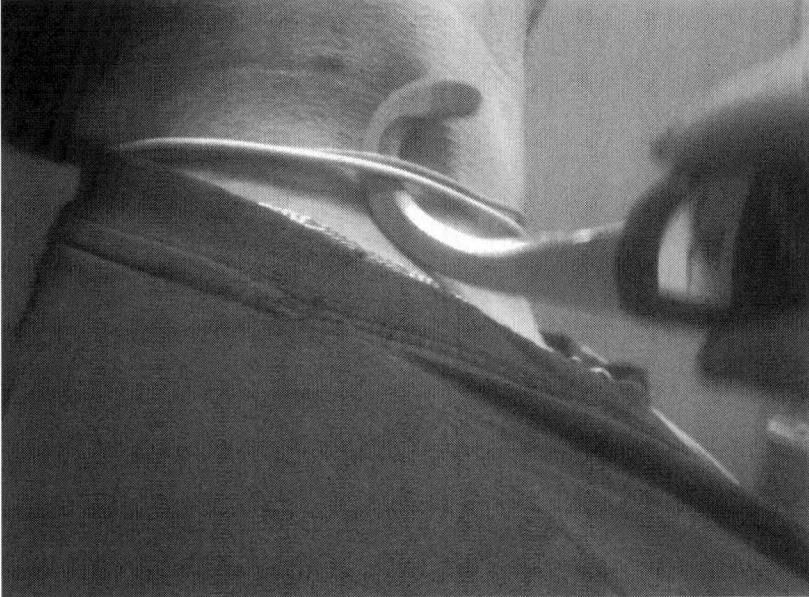

In situations where the person resists actions to remove the ligature, it may be appropriate for staff to restrict the person's ability to struggle, especially where the struggling behaviour increases the risk(s) presented by the ligature, or by the use of the ligature cutter by staff. In such situations, staff should employ appropriate holding skills, sensitive to the needs of the person, in accordance with current practice guidelines and training to facilitate the safe removal of the ligature.

All complete or incomplete suspension incidents must be considered high risk with regard to manual handling, because of the loads involved and possible requirement to adopt awkward postures. Staff should carry out a dynamic risk assessment and apply safe handling principles to the best of their ability in the situations that they find themselves. Staff must not place themselves at unnecessary risk and must not attempt any technique or manoeuvre they feel would be hazardous for them. Where the perceived risks involved with supporting the weight are considered too great, it may be appropriate to cut the ligature and allow the person to fall unhindered to the ground

Complete Suspended Strangulation (hanging)

The priorities are to release the pressure the ligature is causing on the neck and to remove the ligature. Where possible the patient should be elevated by taking a secure hold around the thighs or hips to reduce the tension on the ligature. This can be particularly useful to reduce airway compromise if staff are not able to cut the ligature immediately, and will enable the patient to be supported when the ligature is cut. It may be safest to approach from the front so that the patient will fold towards the shoulder (i.e. towards to handler, and not away from them) after the ligature is cut.

All strangulation attempts should be treated as a suspected spinal injury. Staff should support the neck, as far as is possible. No specific techniques exist to allow for support of the c-spine as the individual is lowered to the ground following hanging, so staff should try to support the head to the best of their ability in the circumstances.

As soon as the body weight is supported, or handlers are clear if the dynamic risk assessment indicates allowing an unhindered drop, the ligature should be cut at a central point between the patient's neck and the suspension point so that there is minimal interference with any potential evidence. If supported, the person should then be lowered to the floor.

If the ligature remains in place around the patient's neck (or other body part) it should be removed using a ligature cutter. Staff should make every effort to cut the ligature at a point that is distant from any knot. Appropriate airway management techniques, to the staff member's level of skill and training, should be applied, mindful of the possibility of spinal injury. An assessment for laryngeal injury should be made as soon as possible by a health care professional.

Incomplete Suspended Strangulation (semi seated or kneeling)

The priorities are to release the pressure the ligature is causing on the neck and to remove the ligature. Where possible, the patient's upper body (and head) should be supported and elevated by taking a secure hold around the upper torso (and head) to reduce the tension on the ligature. This is useful to reduce airway compromise if is not possible to cut the ligature immediately, and will enable the patient to be supported when the ligature is cut.

DO NOT pull on the ligature to remove or unhook it (e.g. – from over a tap or door handle).
As soon as the body weight is supported, or handlers are clear, if the dynamic risk assessment indicates allowing an unhindered drop, the ligature should be cut. Ideally this should be at a central point between the patient's neck and the suspension point. If supported, the person should then be lowered to a supine position, maintaining

manual inline stabilisation of the patient's neck to protect from potential further spinal damage.

Lying Strangulation
Staff should slide the patient towards the point of suspension, using slide sheets if possible, to reduce the tension on the ligature before removal.

Ligature (unsuspended)
The ligature should be removed following the procedure and guidance above.

Following removal of a ligature the patient must be reviewed by a health care professional as clinically indicated, dependent upon the severity of the attempt.

Text Source

Northampton Healthcare (2013) Procedure for the safe use of Ligature Cutters.

Examples of Ligature Removal devices

The Barrington LC1. (www.barringtoninternational.co.uk)

Seatbelt / Ligature cutters

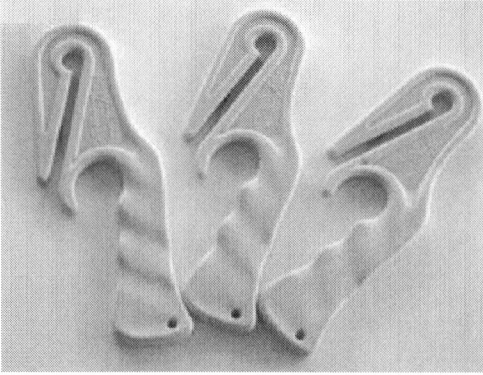

Res-Q-Hook

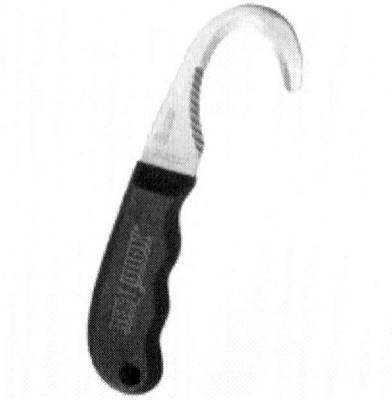

Demonstrate safe use of Automated External Defibrillation (AED).

Defibrillation can be achieved using either an automatic or semi-automatic external defibrillator (AED) or a manual defibrillator. Some AEDs allow you to monitor the patients ECG rhythm. Manual defibrillators can either monitor and advise on shock or allow manual shocks to be delivered. AEDs generally will not allow manual shocks but some designed for professional use do.

The AED will automatically analyse cardiac rhythm (Specificity for recognition of shockable rhythm close to 100%) and prepare for shock delivery.

These devices are getting progressively more common in public places may meaning one is often available. They are also carried on some police support vehicles.

More modern devices use adhesive pads to deliver the shock as this provides better skin contact, as opposed to older models which had paddles, if using paddles apply gel to them before placing on skin.

A defibrillator shock stops the heart allowing its natural pacemaker to take over. Multiple shocks may be needed to achieve this. If using an AED it will determine the required strength of shock required. There are two shockable rhythms Ventricular Fibrillation and Ventricular Tachycardia; knowledge of these are not required as the AED will determine if a shock is required.

During a cardiac arrest the rhythms may change between shockable and non-shockable and the operator must act appropriately.

Before applying defibrillator pads to the patient carry out a primary survey.

- Check for Danger
- Check for Response
- Check for Catasphrophic Bleeding
- Check Airway is Clear
- Check for Breathing
- Check for Circulation

If there is no danger or Catasphrophic Bleeding and insufficient breathing and circulation start CPR and apply AED pads as detailed below.

Danger checks

Ensure there are no immediate threats to yourself.

As an AED delivers an electrical charge care must be taken when treating patient.

Do not administer a shock when someone else is touching the patient.

Do not administer a shock when using a bag valve and mask (BVM) with oxygen near the patient, place the BVM away whilst delivering shock.

Do not use on the Forecourt of Petrol station near pumps.

Do not use in standing water.

Do not use on metal surfaces

Chest Checks

Dry the chest if wet.

Shave if very hairy and pads will not stick to chest.

Avoid any placing pads on any lumps with surgical scars near collar bone as these may be pacemaker sites.

Move or remove any necklaces or jewellery over the chest.

Remove any medication patches from the chest.

Pad positioning

Depending on the manufacture of the AED the pads may have illustrations of positions.

As you are looking at the patient place first pad to the left of Breast Bone (sternum), below the (

Collar bone (clavicle)

Place the second pad on the patient's side in the armpit (mid-axillary line) with the bottom of the pad at the base of the rib cage, clear of breast tissue

Place the axillary electrode pad vertically to improve efficiency

If possible, **continue CPR** whilst the pads are being applied

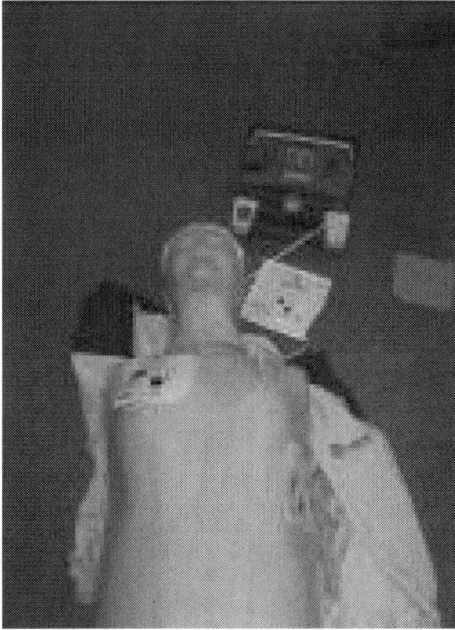

AED Operation

The machine will give audible instructions for the operator to follow such as;

- "Attach pads to patients bear chest"

- "Stand Clear, do not touch the patient, Analysing Heart Rhythm "

- "Shock Advised Charging"

- "Deliver shock now by pressing Red Button"

- "No shock advised, Continue CPR"

The AED will analyse the patient every two minutes and offer appropriate instructions.

Some will provide a clock showing time elapsed and most record the number of shocks that are delivered.

CPR must continue throughout (except when a shock is being delivered) with minimum interruptions.

Children and Defibrillation

Most children; those under 12 years of age will arrest due to a lack of oxygen in their bodies rather than due to heart disease, it is therefore less likely they will have a 'shockable' rhythm. However to maximise their chance of survival the pads should still be applied.

In children use the same positions as for adults except in very young children or infants where placing the pads thus would allow them to touch. In these cases place one on the front and one on the back of the child.

Normal adult pads should be used on children over 8 for younger children paediatric specific pads should be used when available if not use adult pads. The use of AED is not recommended for infants less than 1 year old, however if this is your only choice it can be used.

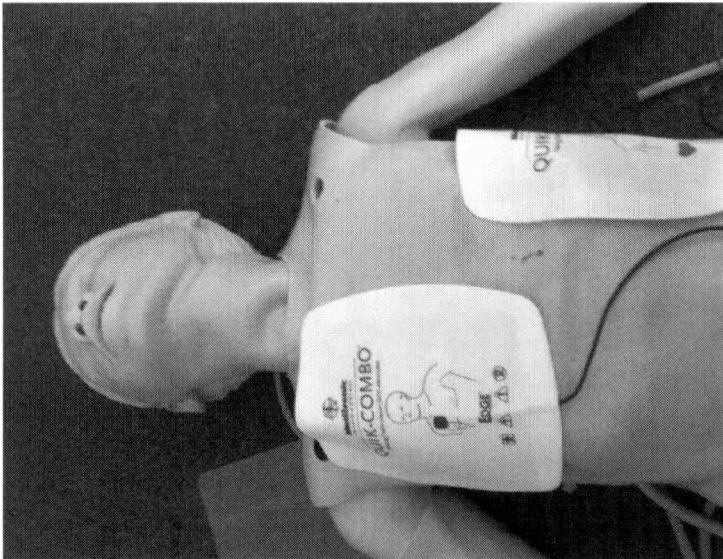

Sequence of actions when using an automated external defibrillator

Adapted from The Resuscitation Council UK (2010) The use of Automated External Defibrillators
http://www.resus.org.uk/pages/aed.pdf

The following sequence applies to the use of both semi-automatic and automatic AEDs in a victim who is found to be unconscious and not breathing normally.

1. Commence CPR, do not delay starting CPR unless the AED is available immediately.

2. As soon as the AED arrives:
- If more than one rescuer is present, continue CPR while the AED is switched on. If you are alone, stop CPR and switch on the AED.
- Follow the voice / visual prompts.
- Attach the electrode pads to the patient's bare chest.
- Ensure that nobody touches the victim while the AED is analysing the rhythm.

3A. If a shock is indicated:
- Ensure that nobody touches the victim.
- Shout "Stand Clear"
- Push the shock button as directed (fully-automatic AEDs will deliver the shock automatically).
- Continue as directed by the voice / visual prompts.
- Minimise, as far as possible, interruptions in chest compression.

3B. If no shock is indicated:
- Resume CPR immediately using a ratio of 30 compressions to 2 rescue breaths.
- Continue as directed by the voice / visual prompts.

4. Continue to follow the AED prompts until:
- Qualified help arrives and takes over OR
- The victim starts to show signs of regaining consciousness, such as coughing, opening his eyes, speaking, or moving purposefully AND starts to breathe normally OR
- You become exhausted.

Triage

The word Triage is derived from the French 'to sort', it has been used in both military and disaster situations to prioritise the treatment of casualties. If the casualty is in cardiac arrest or severely injured and not expected to survive they may be left in favour of casualties that would benefit more from medical attention and evacuation.

In most triage systems casualties are sorted into categories based on an initial survey of their Airway, Breathing and Circulation. When dealing with a mass casualty incident the triage officer will give cards to each casualty showing their Triage Category, there level of consciousness, observations and treatment can be recorded on it. If their condition changes then their Triage Category may also change. The Cards can be folded in different ways to show the various categories.

The initial Sieve is designed to quickly establish priorities a more detailed sort can then take place when resources are available.

The adult Triage Sieve is one method of sorting casualties into one of four categories exist;

Category	Priority	Colour
Delayed	3	Green
Urgent	2	Yellow
Immediate	1	Red
Dead		

Dead

Casualty when checked is not breathing even after opening their airway.

Immediate

Unable to walk & (Respiratory Rate <10 or >29 and/or Central Capillary Refill > 2 seconds)

Urgent

Unable to walk & (Respiratory Rate >9 or <30 and Central Capillary Refill <=2 seconds)

Delayed

Walking Wounded

Triage Sort

The triage sort takes longer to complete as it requires further observations it can change a casualties priority so should be rechecked frequently as resources are available. Total points scored for Glasgow Coma Scale, Respiratory Rate and Systolic Blood Pressure as below.

	GCS		Resps		Systolic BP
4	13-15		10-29		90+
3	9-12		>29		76-89
2	6-8		6-9		50-75
1	4-5		1-5		1-49
0	3		0		0

12   = Priority 3   Delayed

11   = Priority 2   Urgent

<11 = Priority 1   Immediate

0   Dead

Managing Road Traffic Collisions (RTCs)

Your ability to treat casualties at a Road Traffic Collision is both limited by your expertise and equipment that is available. A few general principles apply to most road traffic collisions. If you stop at an accident do so behind the incident blocking the road. Park your vehicle 'defensively' at an angle rather than straight in the road so that if traffic behind you fails to spot the accident and unfortunately hits your vehicle it will not be pushed into the accident causing further injury to the casualties or yourself.

Assess the scene for possible hazards such as fire, fuel spills and hazardous loads. Only approach the scene if it is safe to do so. If it is dark and you have one wear a Hi-viz vest or coat.

Place warning signs and advise control that you require one or more ambulances if casualties are present, update control if you find additional casualties and request support from fire and rescue if casualties are trapped or a fuel spillage is present, if a death has occurred or is likely request support from traffic officers.

If possible approach any vehicle occupants from the front, call out to occupants, say you are there to help and tell them not to move. If they do have a spinal injury the last thing you want them to do is look over their shoulder to see who is approaching behind them.

If the car doors are locked or jammed you may need to gain entry by smashing a window, a rescue hammer is good for this and usually comes with a seatbelt cutter as well.

Ensure you minimise further danger. ALL engines to be switched off, and do not allow people to smoke nearby.

Check that casualties are breathing, if not you need to get them out of the car as quickly as possible to perform CPR, it is extremely difficult to do this when someone is in a vehicle and should only be attempted in situ if they are trapped.

If the casualty is conscious and has suffered any type of head injury or was hit from any side with force, always consider the possibility of a spinal injury and try and encourage them to stay in the car if it is safe to do so.

If possible get them or help them to sit upright and support their head/neck from behind in a neutral position, do not flex the neck if you can help it. You may need to kneel on the backseat of their car to do this effectively, always explain why you are doing things to the casualty as it helps reassure them and calm the situation.

If they are unconscious but breathing insert an oral or nasal airway (if you have them) and open their airway using the Jaw Thrust method if you are trained to do so.

If the occupants are conscious check that they are all accounted for, there have been many cases where unrestrained children and adults have been ejected from vehicles into ditches or over hedges and not immediately been found and babies and small children that were on passengers laps and have been thrown into the foot well. Occupants may have been injured wandered away from the accident then collapsed.

If there are casualties on the road who are not conscious try to get someone to stay with them to monitor their breathing but do not move them unless you have too. If you do not have enough people, try and get them into the recovery position whilst supporting their neck as best as you can to stop it moving about.

The decision as to whether to remove someone from a vehicle can sometimes be difficult to make particularly if you do not have the equipment or personnel to move them safely. If they are not breathing or are in imminent danger then they need to come out quickly.

Other dangers may come from traffic or environmental factors where in your judgement leaving them where they are is more dangerous than moving them. In these situations you need to use common sense.

Placing casualties in a Neutral position keeps the head upright and in line with the spine like a soldier standing to attention and prevents further aggravation to any possible injury sustained in the RTC.

Helmet Removal

If attending a motorcyclist with a full face motorcycle helmet this should only be removed if you can see or suspect a head injury, if the patient is having airway or breathing difficulties or if they are unconscious. To do this safely requires two people.

The first person stabilises the patients head by holding either side of the helmet.

The second person places the thumb and first finger of one hand on the patients cheeks under the helmet and the other hand under the patients neck to support the head.

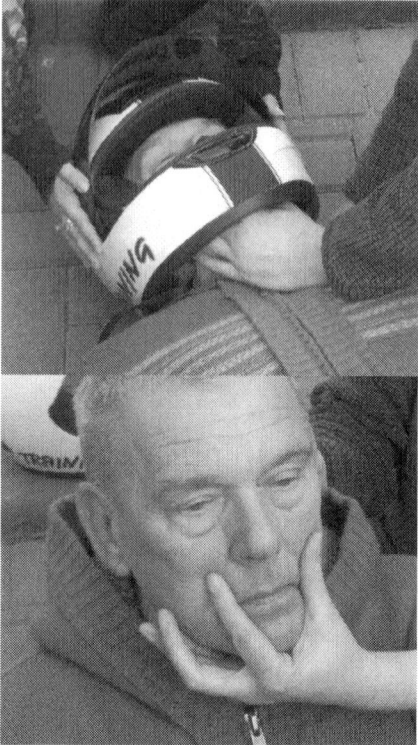

The right hand photo shows finger position without the helmet. To remove helmet the first person, rocks it back and forth to clear the nose and the back of the skull.

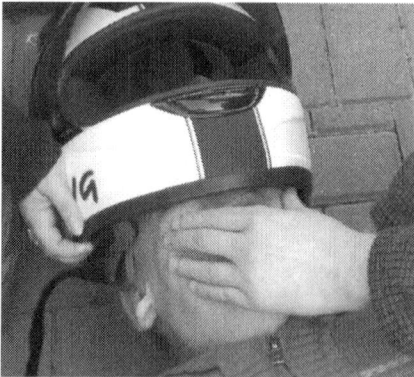

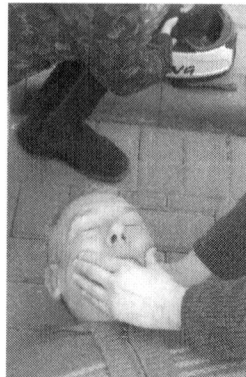

Once the helmet starts to be removed the second person can slide their hand up to support the weight of the head and reposition it in a neutral position.

Managing Environmental Problems

Sunburn

Prevention of sunburn is better than cure, wear loose fitting cool long sleeved tops, wide brimmed hat, sun glasses and a high factor sunscreen. Too much sun can damage the skin, usually it is only superficial but severe sunburn may cause partial thickness burns with blistering. Sunburn can occur on partly cloudy or overcast days when casualties may not be aware of the threat and do not take appropriate precautions

If burnt treat as follows;

- Protect skin from further damage
- Keep in Shade
- Encourage Cool Oral Fluids
- Apply cool moist flannel to affected areas
- Immerse affect parts in cool water

Severe sunburn is commonly underestimated – once blistering has occurred sun burns by definition become a partial thickness burn and need to be managed accordingly.

Heat Exhaustion

Heat exhaustion is caused by loss of water and essential salts from the body. The patient develops a headache and may become dizzy and confused. Show signs of shock including sweating, pale clammy skin, unsteady gait, weakness and fatigue, muscle cramps, nausea, rapid weak pulse and fast breathing. They also may have cramps in limbs and abdomen.

- Keep in Shade
- Encourage sips of Cool Oral Fluids
- Give Rehydration sachets
- Lie down and treat for shock
- Monitor Vital signs

Extreme Heat exhaustion can be life-threatening

Heatstroke

Heatstroke is caused by a long period of heat and can follow on from heat exhaustion and really are part of the same spectrum. Unconsciousness can develop quickly s can convulsions. The patient develops a headache, vomiting and may become dizzy, agitated and confused. Show signs of hot, flushed and dry skin, full bounding pulse and a fever of 40 degrees plus.

Signs of Heat Stroke

- High breathing rate
- Feeling of being hot, uncomfortable
- Low urine output
- Inability to think clearly
- Erratic work pattern
- Fatigue
- Light-headedness or headache
- Nausea
- Muscle cramps
- Sudden rapid increase in pulse rate
- Disorientation, confusion
- Exhaustion
- Collapse
- In very extreme cases death

Treatment

- Keep in Shade
- Encourage sips of Cool Oral Fluids
- Remove outer clothes
- Cool with wet towels, ice or by fanning
- Monitor Vital signs and Temperature

Dehydration

Dehydration like Heat exhaustion is caused by loss of water and essential salts from the body. A person should drink at least 2.5 liters of fluid a day, more in hot climates to replace fluids due to heat and exercise.

The patient develops a headache and may become dizzy, confused, feel nauseous and they may also have cramps in limbs.

- Keep in Shade
- Encourage Oral Fluids
- Give Rehydration sachets
- Stretch and massage areas of cramp
- Monitor Vital signs

Hypothermia

Hypothermia starts when the body's temperature falls below 35 degrees Celsius and can be caused by cold weather or immersion in cold water. A person will begin shivering as the body attempts to generate heat. Their skin becomes cold, pale, dry and they become lethargic. As Hypothermia progresses both breathing and heart rate slow and weaken. Once core temperature falls below 30 Degrees Celsius the patient rarely recovers and may eventually go into respiratory and cardiac arrest.

Signs and Symptoms of Dropping Core Temperature.

°F	°C	Symptoms
98	37	Cold sensations, skin vasoconstriction, increased muscle tension, increased oxygen consumption
97	36	Sporadic shivering suppressed by voluntary movements, gross shivering in bouts, further increase in oxygen consumption, uncontrollable shivering
95	35	Voluntary tolerance limit in laboratory experiments, mental confusion, impairment of rational thought, possible drowning, decreased will to struggle
93	34	Loss of memory, speech impairment, sensory function impairment, motor performance impairment
91	33	Hallucinations, delusions, partial loss of consciousness, shivering impaired
90	32	Heart rhythm irregularities, motor performance grossly impaired
88	31	Shivering stopped, failure to recognize familiar people 86 30 Muscles
86	30	Muscles rigid, no response to pain
84	29	Loss of consciousness
80	27	Ventricular fibrillation (ineffective heartbeat), muscles flaccid
79	26	Death

Protect Casualty from cold, wet and wind

- Prevent further heat loss by changing wet clothing
- Warm them slowly
- Cover with coats, spare blanket or survival bag
- Protect from damp ground
- Give warm drinks and high energy food
- Monitor Vital signs

Frostnip

Frostnip is a more of a temporary discomfort but if left untreated, can eventually turn into frostbite. Usually effects ears, nose or fingers, causes stabbing sharp pain which then becomes red and numb then cold and white, however the skin dose not freeze and remains soft and mobile. To treat slowly reheat, long term problems are rare.

Frostbite

Frostbite occurs when tissues freeze, in severe cases can lead to tissue death and the loss of digits or limbs. Most common in toes, fingers nose and cheeks. First signs are altered sensation 'pin-and-needles' followed by numbness then stiffening of skin. Frostbite can also cause blood poisoning (Septicemia).

- If in fingers, place them somewhere warm like armpits
- Remove gloves, rings etc
- If available, place in warm water 40 Degrees Celsius
- Raise part to reduce swelling

In severe frostbite the toes or fingers may die and dry gangrene can develop. It can take several months to know if frost damaged tissues will live or not.

The chart below shows the drop in temperature when wind is combined with ambient temperature. It also shows time band before you are in danger of frostbite.

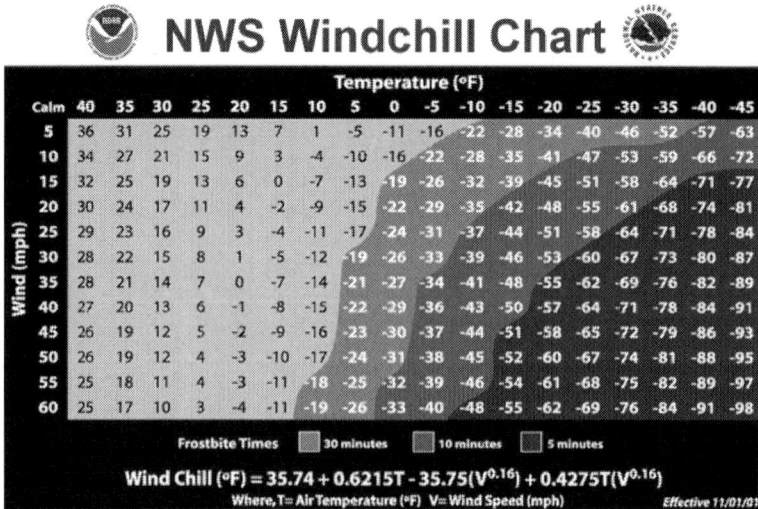

NWS Windchill Chart

							Temperature (°F)										
Calm	40	35	30	25	20	15	10	5	0	-5	-10	-15	-20	-25	-30	-35	-40	-45
5	36	31	25	19	13	7	1	-5	-11	-16	-22	-28	-34	-40	-46	-52	-57	-63
10	34	27	21	15	9	3	-4	-10	-16	-22	-28	-35	-41	-47	-53	-59	-66	-72
15	32	25	19	13	6	0	-7	-13	-19	-26	-32	-39	-45	-51	-58	-64	-71	-77
20	30	24	17	11	4	-2	-9	-15	-22	-29	-35	-42	-48	-55	-61	-68	-74	-81
25	29	23	16	9	3	-4	-11	-17	-24	-31	-37	-44	-51	-58	-64	-71	-78	-84
30	28	22	15	8	1	-5	-12	-19	-26	-33	-39	-46	-53	-60	-67	-73	-80	-87
35	28	21	14	7	0	-7	-14	-21	-27	-34	-41	-48	-55	-62	-69	-76	-82	-89
40	27	20	13	6	-1	-8	-15	-22	-29	-36	-43	-50	-57	-64	-71	-78	-84	-91
45	26	19	12	5	-2	-9	-16	-23	-30	-37	-44	-51	-58	-65	-72	-79	-86	-93
50	26	19	12	4	-3	-10	-17	-24	-31	-38	-45	-52	-60	-67	-74	-81	-88	-95
55	25	18	11	4	-3	-11	-18	-25	-32	-39	-46	-54	-61	-68	-75	-82	-89	-97
60	25	17	10	3	-4	-11	-19	-26	-33	-40	-48	-55	-62	-69	-76	-84	-91	-98

Wind (mph)

Frostbite Times   30 minutes   10 minutes   5 minutes

$$Wind\ Chill\ (°F) = 35.74 + 0.6215T - 35.75(V^{0.16}) + 0.4275T(V^{0.16})$$

Where, T= Air Temperature (°F) V= Wind Speed (mph)

Effective 11/01/01

Chart - http://www.nws.noaa.gov/om/windchill/

Managing Bites and Stings

A number of insects bite or sting, including wasps, bees and ants mosquitoes, midges and some flies and other insects.

Effects vary but the following are common dependant on type;

- Local Irritation and Itching
- Raised reddened lumps
- Swelling
- Possible wound Infections
- Secondary infections transmitted via touch to eyes etc
- Transmission of disease
- Allergic or Anaphylactic reaction

Treatment depends on the severity and the likelihood of infection and complication.

Avoid rubbing and scratching as much as possible as the mechanical act of rubbing or itching causes the release of chemical which makes the bite more itchy and sore. It can also introduce infection into the skin.

Anti-histamine creams are effective but should be used with caution as they can make the skin sensitive to light. For severe or widespread rash the patient should use there own oral anti-histamines.

Cool showers can be useful for cooling the skin, which in turn cools the bite sight and reduces itch.

If a patient shows signs such as breathing problems or loss of consciousness treat for anaphylaxis.

Managing Infestation

Various types of infestations exist;

Scabies

Scabies is a contagious skin infection that effects humans and other animals and is caused by a mite that burrows under the skin, causing itching and a rash.

Infection can be transferred via fabric or directly from another host and has an incubation period of 4-6 weeks. Although if cured and re-infected itching can start again within a 2-3 days. However, throughout this time, you can infect other people. Unfortunately symptoms continue for a period after mites have been killed. Infected areas often include areas between fingers, toes and in skin folds, around the genital area, buttocks and under the breasts of women. The pattern of mites burrows show as straight or s-shaped tracks in the skin, often with rows of small bites.

It is treated with a variety of creams available from chemists

In order to prevent re-infection, the patient's family and any others who have had skin to skin contact must also be treated at the same time.

Do not wash prior to applying treatment, apply to the whole body including the scalp, face, neck and ears, but avoid mucous membranes (i.e. eyes, inside the nose, or mouth).

Pay particular attention to behind the ears.

Rub into the webs of the fingers and toes, underneath the nails.

Treat the soles of the feet.

Follow manufacturer's instructions for length of time of application.

Repeat the treatment one week later.

Lice

Lice that effect humans come in three types;

Head Lice which are transmitted by close contact,

Patient will be itchy and both eggs and lice will be visible. Treat with repeated insecticide lotions and fine combing, promote clean hair.

Body lice spread by poor hygiene

Patient will be itchy, both eggs and lice will be visible on clothes and/or skin. Burn or sterilise clothes, bathe with soap and 1% Lysol.

Pubic Lice (Crab Lice) spread by sexual contact.

Infects all body hair, causes bluish staining and itching.

Treat Pubic Lice with repeated insecticide lotions and fine combing, and promote good hygiene

Lice eggs (nits) are oval, yellowish-white in colour, are hard to see and may be confused with dandruff. They take about a week to hatch. The empty egg cases remain after hatching.

Nymphs hatch from the nits. The baby lice look like the adults, but are smaller. They take about 7 days to mature to adults and feed on blood to survive.

Adults can live up to 30 days and feed on blood. Head lice cannot jump, hop or swim.

The itch takes from one week to 2-3 months to develop. Itching may also occur due to an allergic reaction to the bites. Sores can develop due to scratching the bites which can then become infected.

Fleas

Patients can be infected by both human and animal fleas. Their bites show in small groups and are very itchy.

Threadworms (pinworms)

Threadworms are white cotton like worms found on the skin around anus or in stools. They cause anal irritation and discomfort. When the person scratches the area the eggs are transferred via the fingernails to the mouth and swallowed. They can also be picked up from infected clothes and linen.

- Sign and symptoms
- Seeing worms, (which appear like threads) on the anus, or in the faeces
- Itching, redness and soreness around the anus
- Irritability
- Disturbed sleep

All members of a family or group should be treated.

Worms only live for around 6 weeks and good hygiene should prevent re-infection or cross infection. Washing, vacuuming and discouraging scratching is the best way to stop spread. In very rare cases they may cause Appendicitis

Bed Bugs

Bed bugs do not fly, but can move very quickly. They are nocturnal, and feed at night. They can be found in crevices and cracks in wallpaper, furniture, bed frames and mattresses, even in clothes.

They are difficult to kill, bedding should be washed at the highest temperature for the fabric, and tumble dried on a high setting. Thoroughly vacuum mattresses and steam clean carpets. Powerful chemicals will be required.

Red weal's will appear, which are very itchy, and are often in an orderly row. Occasionally, blisters may form with swelling around the bite.

Although unpleasant, they do not carry disease. But if you are bitten and then scratch the area, this could introduce bacteria from under your nails into the wound.

Entonox

A mix of 50% Oxygen and 50% nitrous oxide is both an analgesic and anaesthetic gas. Used in dentistry, child birth and emergency medicine. It is fast acting taking around 3-5 minutes to take effect and 5-10 minutes for maximum effect. It is self-administered and the patient must inhale deeply to operate the demand valve.

It can be delivered through a mouth piece or facemask and maximum effect is gained when the patient breathes in and out whilst keeping the mouthpiece or mask against or in the mouth.

When taken properly can be effective as opiates.

Exclusions
- Violently disturbed psychiatric patients.

- Severe head injuries with a changed level of consciousness.

- Anyone who has been diving within 24 hours as they may have decompression sickness which entonox will worsen.

Cautions
Penetrating torso injury, where punctured lung or bowel is suspected.

Side effects
Euphoria, disorientation, sedation, nausea, vomiting, dizziness and generalised tingling are common and generally minor and rapidly reversible.

Capacity, Consent and Documentation

Capacity / Consent

Before giving any treatment consent must if possible should be obtained either verbally or by intonation I.e. If you tell the patient you are going to take their pulse and they offer you their arm they don`t also need to say go ahead as they are implying their consent. If they crossed their arms and moved away you can assume they are not consenting to that act.

In order to give informed consent they must be fully aware of what you intend to do and the consequences if any for themselves.

In order to demonstrate capacity;

- They must be able to understand what you are telling them
- Retain the information,
- Make a decision
- Communicate it back to you.

If they unable to do any part of this then they lack the capacity to consent in which case as a care giver you must act on the patients best interest.

Documentation

When providing care it is important to document all treatment given. In normal situations this is often done in an accident book which records biographical details I.e. Name, address, date of birth, doctor etc followed by the nature and history of the accident or illness then details of treatments given and if the patient attended hospital or doctor. Any medical Documentation acts as a record for legal purposes.

Psychological Problems

Psychological stress is likely to be a major problem following any tragic situation and within the context of that there are a number of obvious stressors:

Deaths or serious injuries of friends / family

Fear at possible outcomes

Grief at loss of "life-style" or changes to plans or expectations

Constant high level stress

Situational crisis such as this can also bring any pre-existing psychological disorder on – depression, psychosis, anxiety, obsessive compulsive disorder.

Depression

This is big catch-all term with lots of subgroups within it – essentially it is low mood – but spectrum from feeling sad to being trapped in black hole with no hope and no pleasure from life.

There true clinical term applies to those at the more severe end of the spectrum and this is the end of the spectrum we are primarily talking about here. Major depression is characterised by feelings of hopelessness / low mood combined with a combination off:

- Poor sleep
- Poor appetite
- Lack of enjoyment or pleasure in life / sadness
- Moodiness
- Fatigue
- Feelings of worthlessness
- Inability to concentrate

The less severe end of the spectrum is really not a lot different to an unhappiness with life – a significant number of people are unhappy with life, work, partners or friends and this will be exaggerated in a catastrophe. But this is not true depression and it is important to make a distinction. Many people have found themselves on anti-depressants simply due to being unhappy with life and being unwilling or unable to make required changes to their lives. For these people generally support and a degree of understanding from their family group and friends will go a long way.

Suicide prevention

In situations of high stress it is important to have an increased awareness of the possibility of suicide. Early intervention with recognition and emotional support will frequently help. Ultimately if someone is determined to take their own life it is often very difficult to stop.

The pneumonic SAD PERSONS provides a way to remember risk factors:

S – sex – male

A – age – older

D – depression – history of

P – previous attempts

E – ethanol abuse – heavy alcohol drinking

R – rational thinking loss – is unable to see things in a rational way

S – support – lack of

O – Organised plan – of how they would do it

N – No spouse or partner

S – Sickness – being chronically or disabling unwell

To assess a patients risk of self-harm or suicide a number of tools exist. Using the facts below add I pt for each fact present. Less than 3 indicate a low risk, 3-6 a medium risk, 7+ High Risk

- Patient is Male
- Age under 19
- Aged over 45
- History of Depression
- Previous self-Harm
- High Alcohol / Drug Use
- Loss of Rational thinking
- Widowed, Divorced or Separated
- Serious attempt at Suicide or Self Harm
- No close family, friends or job
- Determined to Repeat attempts
- Ambivalent when questioned

Psychosis

Psychosis is an abnormal perception of stimulus / loss of contact with reality

A common feature are hallucinations – auditory and or visual.

It is a spectrum from a single episode (more common) to being a component of a broader illness such as schizophrenia, bipolar disorder or severe depression. Regardless of the under lying biochemical cause it can be precipitated by drug abuse, severe stress / exposure to psychological trauma, sleep depression

The diagnostic criteria are very variable and complex, but the basics of this diagnosis is the loss of touch with reality.

Dealing with someone who is psychotic can be very distressing to carers. It is also very disabling to the patient. The basic management of psychosis is aimed at calming the patients and frequent tethering to reality. The main elements can be paranoia or aggression which may place you in danger.

Most episodes self-limiting and can be managed with support and minimising the stimulus which lead to the psychosis – drugs, alcohol, stress.

Recurrent or persistent psychosis is much more of a problem. Historically "madness" or "insanity" wasn't uncommon and while this was a catch-all for a lot of illnesses a number would have been psychotic.

Reactions to loss and grief

Elizabeth Kubler-Ross in 1969 published a book on death and dying in it she discussed the stages people go through when coming to terms with an impending death usually from a terminal disease. Although her work has been disputed since that time, the basic principles are widely accepted.

The same model of loss and grief can be applied to someone left behind after the death of a relative or close friend and also to someone who is involved in a tragic situation.

The model consists of five stages there is no set sequence in which they may be experienced and a person may not experience all the stages or may move back and forth between stages as mood and experience change.

Denial

Where the person won't believe the situation applies to them.

Anger

The beginning of acceptance of the situation, the person becomes angry that the situation has happened to them. Feelings of anger and envy for those in a better position become evident.

Bargaining

In this stage the person try`s to negotiate to extend own or others life sometimes using religion as a support.

Depression

This is a feeling of hopelessness, it may bring on suicidal thoughts and the person detaches themselves from those around them.

Acceptance

The final stage when the person accepts the inevitable and both physically and mentally prepares for it.

Dementia

Dementia is an umbrella term used to describe a group of symptoms exhibited by patients with Alzheimer's, vascular dementia, picks disease, lewy bodies, Parkinson's and CJD. The symptoms of CJD do not occur for decades, so consequently the amount of cases that will arise from the BSE crisis of the 1990s is not yet known. Dementia is a progressive degeneration of the brain which commonly affects the speech and language centres, thus patient's often loose short and or long term memory, have difficulty understanding speech and communicating. They also can lose life skills such being able to care for themselves.

Statistically the likelihood of developing dementia doubles every 5 years after 65. By the age of 85, 20% of the population will have it.

There is no cure for dementia and it is a fatal disease usually within 10 years of first developing symptoms. However there are thought to be protective measures which will decrease the chance of developing it.

Meningitis

Meningitis is an infection of the covering of the brain. Also possible are brain abscess or infection in the brain itself(encephalitis). Consider this diagnosis if severe headache and high temperature and has an aversion to light (Photophobia), a stiff neck, muscle aches and back ache.

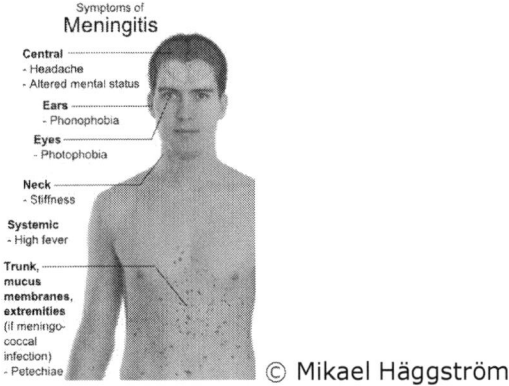

Symptoms of
Meningitis

Central
- Headache
- Altered mental status

Ears
- Phonophobia

Eyes
- Photophobia

Neck
- Stiffness

Systemic
- High fever

Trunk,
mucus
membranes,
extremities
(if meningo-
coccal
infection)
- Petechiae

© Mikael Häggström

Commonly Prescribed medication

It is beyond the scope of this book to go into detail on each drug, so information leaflets must be studied carefully and it is recommended you also purchase a reliable up to date Pharmacy Book, In the UK the British National Formulary (BNF) is published twice a year and is an excellent resource.

I'm constantly amazed at the number of patients I visit that when asked what past medical history or problems they have, claim to have none or very few, but when looking at their prescriptions they are taking a considerable amount of medication.

So why is this, I believe it is due to a number of factors;

Patients don`t consider a condition to be a problem if it is well controlled, such as Hypertension or Diabetes.

Patients are unaware of exactly why a doctor may have prescribed a particular medication as they 'trust' them to do the right thing.

They may be embarrassed by a particular problem such as urinary incontinence or fungal infections and not mention them.

Practically all drugs have one or more potential side effects in some cases they may be unpleasant such as causing diarrhoea or dizziness. But contrary to popular belief not all medication is harmful if taken in excess.

Medication which has a sedation effect, lowers blood pressure or alters pulse rate or rhythm may itself be the cause or contributing factor to why the patient has called for assistance.

In the table below you will find a selection of the 300+ most prescribed medications and their common use. In some cases both generic and common brand names are listed to aid identification. Always check with the patient the listed use is what is intended for that patient, as some have multiple uses that are less common.

Drug Name	Uses
Aciclovir	Antiviral, Herpes
Adalat	(See Nifedipine)
Adcal-D3	Calcium supplement
Adipine	(See Nifedipine)
Adizem-XL	(See diltiazem)
Alendronic Acid	Osteoporosis
Alfacalcidol	Vitamin D deficiency, Kidney
Alfuzosin	retention, incontinence, Prostate
Allopurinol	Gout, Kidney stones
Alverine Citrate	IBS, diverticula or painful periods
Aminophylline	Bronchodilator
Amiloride	Hypertension, CHF
Amisulpride	Antipsychotic, Depression
Amitriptyline	Anxiety, depression, pain
Amiodarone	Abnormal heart rhythms
Amlodipine	Angina
Amoxicillin	Antibiotic
Anastrozole	Breast Cancer
Aricept	Alzheimer's disease.
Arimidex	Breast Cancer
Arthrotec	Diclofenac/Misoprostol (NSAID)
Asacol	Ulcerative colitis, Crohn's disease
Asasantin Ret	Anti-thrombolytic
Aspirin	Antiplatelet, Anti-Pyretic, Analgesia
Atenolol	Hypertension
Azathioprine	Immunosuppressive
Atorvastatin	Lowering blood cholesterol
Baclofen	MS, Alcoholism
Bendroflumethiazide	Diuretic, Hypertension
Betahistine	Anti-vertigo, Balance Problems
Bezafibrate	Hyperlipidaemia
Bisacodyl	Constipation, Bowel Dysfunction

Bisoprolol Fumar	Hypertension
Bumetanide	Diuretic, Heart failure
Buprenorphine	Addiction, Pain
Buccastem	Nausea, Vertigo, Antipsychotic
Buscopan	abdominal cramps
Calc & Ergocalciferol	Calcium & Vitamin D
Calc & Colecal	Calcium
Calc Carb_Tab Chble	Calcium
Calceos	Calcium
Calcichew	Calcium
Candesartan Cilexetil	Hypertension
Carbamazepine	Epilepsy, bipolar disorder, Pain
Carbimazole	Hyperthyroidism.
Carbocisteine	Reduces the viscosity of sputum
Carvedilol	Congestive heart failure.
Cefaclor	Antibiotic
Cefalexin	Antibiotic
Cefradine	Antibiotic
Celecoxib	(NSAID)
Cerazette	Contraceptive
Cetirizine	Antihistamine
Chlordiazepoxide	Sedative
Chlorphenamine	Antihistamine
Chlorpromazine	Antipsychotic
Cilest	Contraceptive
Cinnarizine	Antihistamine, Nausea & Vomiting
Ciprofloxacin	Antibiotic
Citalopram	Depression
Clarithromycin	Antibiotic
Clobazam	Seizures
Clomipramine	Tricyclic antidepressant
Clonazepam	anticonvulsant, muscle relaxant
Clonidine	Hypertension, Pain, Insomnia

Clopidogrel	Antiplatelet
Co-Amilofruse	Diuretic
Co-Amilozide	Hypertension, CHF
Co-Amoxiclav	Antibiotic
Co-Codamol	Codeine/Paracetamol Analgesia
Co-Cyprindiol	Prostate problems
Co-Careldopa	Parkinsons
Co-Dydramol	Dihydrocodeine & paracetamol
Co-Fluampicil	Antibiotic
Co-Proxamol	Paracetamol & Aspirin, Analgesia
Co-Tenidone	Hypertension
Codeine Phosphate	Analgesia
Coracten XL	(see Nifedipine)
Creon 10000	Assists digestion
Cyanocobalamin	pernicious anemia; vit B_{12} deficiency
Cyclizine	Nausea & Vomiting
Desloratadine	Antihistamine
Desogestrel	Contraceptive
Detrusitol	Urinary incontinence.
Dexamethasone	Anti-Inflammatory
Dianette	Prostate disorders
Diazepam	Anxiety, insomnia, seizures
Diclofenac	Analgesia
Digoxin	Atrial fibrillation, Atrial flutter
Dihydrocodeine	Analgesia
iltiazem	Hypertension, Angina, Arrhythmia
Dipyridamole	Anti-thrombolytic
Docusate Sod	Laxatives, Stool softener
Domperidone	Nausea and Vomiting

Drug	Use
Donepezil	Alzheimer's disease.
Dosulepin	tricyclic antidepressant
Doxazosin	Hypertension, Urinary retention
Doxycycline	Antibiotic
Duloxetine	Depression
Dutasteride	Prostatic problems
Enalapril	Hypertension
Epanutin	Antiepileptic.
Epilim Chrono 500	Anticonvulsant
Eprosartan	Hypertension
Erythromycin	Antibiotic
Escitalopram	Anti-depressant
Esomeprazole	Peptic Ulcer / GORD
Ethinylestradiol	Contraceptive
Etodolac	NSAID
Etoricoxib	Anti-Inflammatory
Exemestane	Breast cancer
Ezetimibe	High cholesterol
Felodipine	Hypertension
Femodene	Contraceptive
Femulen	Contraceptive
Fenofibrate	High cholesterol
Ferrous Fumar	Iron deficiency anemia
Ferrous Gluconate	Iron deficiency anemia
Ferrous Sulphate	Iron deficiency anemia
Fexofenadine	Antihistamine
Finasteride	Prostate Problems
Flecainide Acet	Anti Arrhythmic
Flucloxacillin	Antibiotic
Fluoxetine	Ant Depressant
Folic Acid	Vitamin B
Forceval	Multi-vitamins

Fosamax	Osteoporosis
Fluconazol	Fungal Infections
Fludrocort Acet	Addison's Disease
Furosemide	Diuretic
Gabapentin	neuropathic pain, fibromyalgia
Gaviscon Advance	GERD
Glibenclamide	Diabetes
Gliclazide	Diabetes
Glimepiride	Diabetes
Glipizide	Diabetes
Glucophage SR	Diabetes
Glucosamine	Osteoarthritis
Glyceryl Trinitrate	Angina
Half-Indera	Anxiety

Drug Name	Uses
Haloperidol	Aantipsychotic
Hydrocortisone	Steroid
Hydroxocobalamin	Vitamin B12
Hydroxychloroquinine	Rheumatic
Hydroxyzine	Antihistamine
Hyoscine Butylbrom	Biliary Colic
Ibandronic Acid	Osteoporosis
Ibuprofen	Anti-Inflammatory
ICaps	Multi Vitamins
Imdur Durule	Angina
Imipramine	Anti depressant
Indapamide	Hypertension, Cardiac Failure
Indometacin	NSAID
Indoramin	Hypertension
Irbesartan	Hypertension
Isosorbide Mononitrate	Angina
Isotard 60 XL	Angina
Itraconazole	Fungal Infection
Kapake	(see co-codamol)
Lacidipine	Hypertension
Lamotrigine	anticonvulsant
Lansoprazole	Ulcers, GERD
Lercanidipine	Hypertension
Letrozole	Breast Cancer
Levetiracetam	Epilepsy
Levocetirizine	Antihistamine
Levonorgestrel	Contraceptive
Levothyroxine	Hypothyroid
Lisinopril	Hypertension, CHF
Lithium Carbonate	Depression
Loestrin 20	Contraceptive
Lofepramine	Anti depressant

Logynon	Contraceptive
Loperamide	Anti diarrheal
Loratadine	Antihistamine
Lorazepam	Anxiety, Sedation
Losartan Potassium	Hypertension
Lymecycline	Antibiotic
Marvelon	Contraceptive
Mebeverine	Irritable bowel syndrome
Mefenamic Acid	NSAID
Mepradec	Indigestion
Mercilon	Contraceptive
Mesalazine	ulcerative colitis
Metformin	Diabetes
Meloxicam	NSAID
Methadone	Opioids Substitute

Drug Name	Uses
Methotrexate	Ectopic Pregnancy, Abortion
Metoclopramide	Nausea and vomiting
Metoprolol Tart	Hypertension, CHF
Metronidazole	Antibiotic
Microgynon 30	Contraceptive
Micronor	Contraceptive
Minocycline	Antibiotic
Mirtazapine	Antidepressant
Montelukast	Hay Fever, Asthma
Monomax XL	Angina
Morphine Sulphate	Analgesia
Moxonidine	Hypertension
Mst Continus	Analgesia
Naftidrofuryl Oxal	Circulatory Problems
Naproxen	NSAID
Naratriptan	Migraine
Nebivolol	Hypertension
Nefopam	Analgesia
Nicorandil	Analgesia
Nifedipine	Hypertension, Angina
Nitrazepam	Sedative
Nitrofurantoin	Antibiotic, UTI
Norethisterone	Contraceptive. Breast Cancer
Noriday	Contraceptive
Nortriptyline	Antidepressant
Olanzapine	Antipsychotic
Olmesartan	Hypertension
Omacor	Fish Oil
Omeprazole	Indigestion, peptic Ulcer
Orlistat	Obesity
Ovranette	Contraceptive
Oxazepam	Sedative, Anxiety, depression

Oxybutynin	Urinary and bladder difficulties
Oxytetracycline	Antibiotic
Pantoprazole	GORD
Paracetamol	Analgesia
Paracetamol/Tramadol	Analgesia
Paroxetine	Antidepressant
Pentasa	Ulcerative colitis, Crohn's
Perindopril Erbumine	Hypertension, Heart Failure
Peppermint Oil	IBS
Phenobarbital	Sedative
Phenoxymethylpenicillin	Antibiotic
Phenytoin	antiepileptic
Phyllocontin Continus	bronchodilator
Pioglitazone	Diabetes
Piriton	Antihistamine

Drug Name	Uses
Pizotifen Malate	Migraine
Pravastatin	High Cholesterol
Prednisolone	Steroid
Pregabalin	Anticonvulsant
Premarin	HRT
Priadel	Bipolar disorder, depression
Prochlpzine Mal	Nausea, anti psychotic
Procyclidine	Parkinson's disease
Promethazine	Antihistamine
Propranolol	Hypertension
Pseudoephed	Decongestant
Quetiapine	antipsychotic
Quinine Bisulph	Cramps
Quinine Sulphate	Cramps, Malaria
Rabeprazole Sodium	Ulcers, GERD
Raloxifene	Osteoporosis
Ramipril	Hypertension, Heart Failure
Ranitidine	Peptic Ulcer
Risedronate	Osteoporosis
Risperidone	Antipsychotic
Rizatriptan	Migraine
Rosiglitazone	Diabetes
Rosuvastatin	High Cholesterol
Salazopyrin	Lower Bowel Inflammatory Disease
Senna	Laxative
Sertraline	antidepressant
Sibutramine	appetite suppressant
Sildenafil	erectile dysfunction
Simvador	High Cholesterol
Simvastatin	High Cholesterol
Sinemet-Plus	Parkinson's disease
Sitagliptin	Diabetes

Sodium Bicarbonate	Antacid
Sodium Valproate	Anticonvulsant
Solifenacin	Overactive Bladder
Solpadol	(see Co-codamol)
Sotalol	Hypertension, arrhythmias
Spironol	Diuretic
Spasmonal	GI Muscle Relaxant
Sulfasalazine	Arthritis
Sumatriptan	Migraine
Sulpiride	Antipsychotic
Tabphyn	Prostate, Urinary Retention
Tadalafil	Erectile dysfunction
Tamoxifen Cit	Breast Cancer
Tamsulosin	Prostate, Urinary Retention
Tegretol Ret	seizures, nerve pain, bipolar disorder
Tibolone	osteoporosis
Tildiem	Hypertension, Arrhythmia, Angina
Telmisartan	Hypertension
Temazepam	Sedative
Terbinafine	Fungal nail infections
Thiamine	Vitamin B
Tolterodine	Urinary incontinence
Tramadol	Analgesia
Tranexamic Acid	Prevents Blood Clots
Trazodone	Antidepressant
Trifluoperazine	Antidepressant
Trimethoprim	Antibiotics
Trospium Chlor	Urinary retention and incontinence
Tylex	See Co-codamol
Uniphyllin Continus	Bronchodilator
Valsartan	Hypertension, CHF
Varenicline Tart	smoking cessation
Venlafaxine	Antidepressant

Verapamil	Hypertension, Anginaa
Warfarin	anticoagulant.
Xismox	Angina
Yasmin	Contraceptive
Zapain	(See Co-Codamol)
Zolmitriptan	Migraine
Zolpidem Tart	Sedative
Zopiclone	Sedative

Recording a Blood Pressure

The first higher figure (Systolic) is the pressure of blood leaving the heart; the second lower figure (Diastolic) is the pressure of blood in your arteries between heart beats. Blood Pressure is measured as millimetres of mercury, expressed as mmHg

An average normal adult has a blood pressure of 120/70 mmHg. As we get older our blood pressure tends to rise. The treatment threshold at which patients are Hypertensive (have High Blood Pressure) and are usually medicated is 140/85 mmHg. Pressures between 120/70 mmHg and 140/85 mmHg are referred to as pre-hypertensive blood pressures, and above 140/85 mmHg as Hypertensive pressures. People who have had a stroke, heart attack, have coronary Artery disease (CHD) or diabetes should maintain their blood pressure below 130/80 mmHg.

Blood Pressure for Children varies as follows:

New Born	Systolic 70-90	Diastolic 45
6 Months	Systolic 70-90	Diastolic 55
1 Years	Systolic 70-90	Diastolic 60
2-4 Years	Systolic 80-100	Diastolic 60
6-8 Years	Systolic 90-110	Diastolic 60
10-12 Years	Systolic 90-110	Diastolic 65
14 Years	Systolic 100-120	Diastolic 65

Ultimately people die due to decreased cerebral perfusion, which is a decrease in the amount of oxygen going to their brain. This is generally caused by clinical shock which itself has a number of causes and is discussed in more detail in the chapter on shock.

Hypovalemia - Loss of Blood, plasma or severe dehydration

Cardiogenic – Damage to the heart

Obstructive - Damage to the heart or Lungs

Septic – Bacterial, viral, fungal infections

Neurogenic – Due to head or spinal injury

Anaphylactic – Due to vasodilatation , blood vessels getting bigger

To measure blood pressure you either need a manual or automatic sphygmomanometer. Automatic ones can be affected by a number of things, so best practice is to use a manual one.

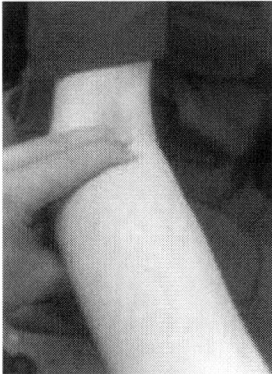

Apply the cuff of the sphygmomanometer to the upper arm

Straighten arm with palm up

Feel for the brachial pulse on the inside of the elbow

Close the valve

Inflate until you can no longer feel the pulse then increase by 30mmHg

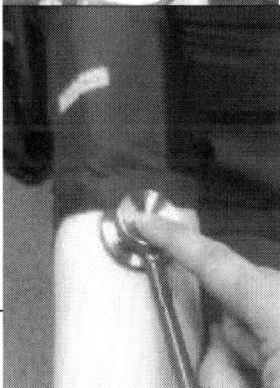

Place the stethoscope over the pulse

Open the valve then slowly release the air.

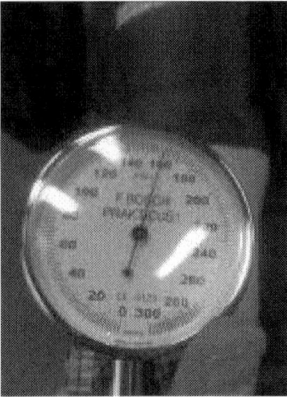

Listen for the sound of blood passing through the vessel (systolic)(thump-thump-thump)

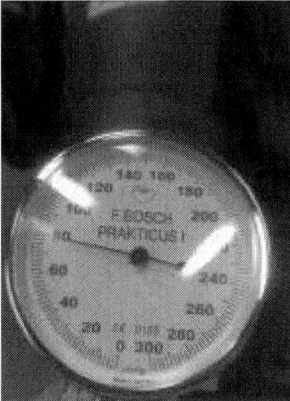

Listen for when it stops. (Diastolic)

Obstetrics and Gynaecology

It is really important to have a good understand of obstetrics and gynaecology.

The Pregnant Patient

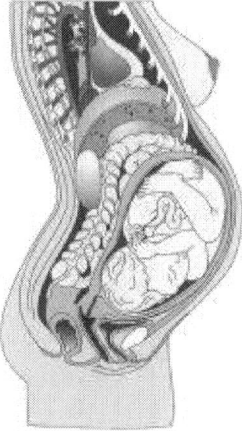

© Maryna Melnyk | Dreamstime.com

The female body goes through many changes when pregnant. Anatomical changes make managing the airway more challenging. They are more prone to gastric reflux of acid and other stomach contents. Changes in shape of the ribs and physiological changes make them mildly breathless and increase respiration rate. The heart enlarges which can make their ECG appear abnormal and they are often mildly anaemic. Systolic BP is slightly reduced with a larger decrease in diastolic BP.

Due to the size and position of the uterus when the patient lies flat the blood returning to the heart is reduced due to compression of the vena cava. Therefore the patient should be laid leaning to the left (Left Lateral Position) with support under the right buttock.

As they have a larger blood volume for them and the baby, signs of haemorrhage and shock won't start until they have lost a third of their blood volume by which time both will be in serious trouble.

The diagnosis of pregnancy

Urine pregnancy test

Test's for the presence of a hormone produced in the early placental tissue – HCG. These test kits are small, lightweight and cheap; and worth stocking up on.

Clinical

The clinical diagnosis of pregnancy is usually a combination of things:- a missed period (or 2), trying to get pregnant or "feels pregnant" (sore breasts, unexplained nausea)

When is the baby due?

The baby is due approximately 288 days from the patients last period (LMP) - (LMP + 15 days) – 3 months. E.g. (1st April + 15 days) – 3 months = 16th January

Early pregnancy problems

Miscarriage

Around 4 in 10 women experience bleeding or cramping within the first 20 weeks of pregnancy, this is best treated with limited rest. 2 in 10 women will abort the foetus within this period and there is nothing that can be done to prevent it.

If the foetus and afterbirth are all passed the pain and bleeding will stop. In some women the bleeding will be torrential – this is likely due to the afterbirth becoming stuck in the cervix – it can be removed with your fingers. This will usually stop heavy bleeding. Low level bleeding for several weeks in inconvenient but will usually stop by itself.

Ectopic Pregnancy

An ectopic pregnancy is one which implants and starts to grow anywhere but in the uterus (where it is supposed to be) – most commonly in a fallopian tube and erodes blood vessels and causes the tube to rupture.

The pain is classically unilateral pain +/- vaginal bleeding in someone who is 8-14 weeks pregnant. They may present with shoulder pain and abdominal pain – which is classical "referred" pain and is due to blood running in the abdominal cavity upwards to the diaphragm and causing irritation (which is felt as shoulder pain)

The diagnosis in hospital is by blood test (measuring the HCG hormone) and ultrasound. Neither of which are commonly available in an austere situation.

Ante-partum problems (problems after 20 weeks)

Placenta Praevia

When the placenta implants near or across the cervical opening. There are several degrees and in the milder forms the mother may be able to push the baby past and out – provided blood loss can be managed in labour.

Symptoms: painless. Heavy bleeding after 24 weeks.

Treat in left lateral position, support ABC, urgent caesarean section.

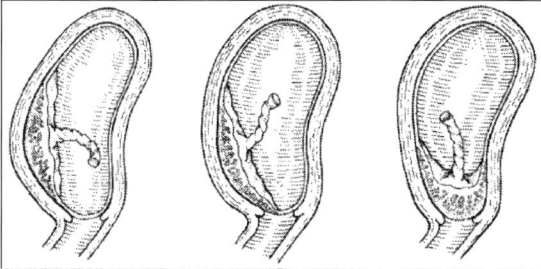
©WHO(2003)P.236

Placenta Abruption

This occurs when placenta partially separates from the wall of the uterus causing heavy bleeding. There are milder forms where just a tiny fraction separates and bleed is light and self-limiting. For the remainder if delivery is not imminent then caesarean is the only option to save mother and baby.

Symptoms: lower abdominal pain, vaginal haemorrhage, uterus tender and rigid, sign of shock, reduced/absent foetal movement or heartbeat.

Treat in left lateral position, support ABC, keep nil by mouth (NBM), urgent caesarean section.

Pre-Eclampsia

This is a unique disease of pregnancy. It is a disease of abnormal placental implantation. The disease itself is complex, but the outcome is high blood pressure, leaky kidneys (protein in the urine) and oedema (extra fluid in the tissues leading to swollen ankles and hands).

Symptoms: Over 20 weeks gestation and diastolic BP>95mmHg or BP>140/90. You also can see swelling (due to oedema) and in severe cases; upper abdominal pain, headache and visual disturbance. If untreated it can lead to inter-uterine death and/or eclampsia.

Eclampsia

This is fitting in Pregnancy, occurring as a consequence of pre-eclampsia and due to High Blood Pressure.

Treatment: Manage in the left lateral position, give oxygen if available

The treatment for severe pre-eclampsia and eclampsia is delivery of the baby. If not already well established labour caesarean section in the option of last resort.

Pre-term labour

This is labour before 38 weeks. Survival after 34 is likely. They need to be kept warm and fed with breast milk if possible (may need via NGT). The odd one will die. Survival before 30 weeks is unlikely and realistically the baby will die. The grey zone is between 30-34 weeks – the majority will probably die from respiratory problems. However some babies will not have respiratory problems and provided they are kept warm and can be fed they may well survive. The administration of steroids (Betnesol is the best, but any steroid will do – 2 doses, 24 hours apart) will improve fatal lung development and may enhance their survival.

Child Birth

Normal Labour

There are three stages of labour

First stage – from the establishment of regular contractions with dilation of the cervix to full dilation

Second stage – from full dilation to delivery of the baby

Third Stage – from delivery of the baby to delivery of the placenta.

With each stages comes possible problems and complications and we have addressed these at each stage.

First Stage of labour

This is from the establishment of regular contractions (2-3 minutes) that cause changes to the cervix (you need both to be in labour). It can be associated with a 'show' of blood stained mucus, rupture of the membranes and descent of the head into the pelvis.

The initial flattening (effacement) of the cervix and the first 3cm dilation can take several hours to a day, but after that it should progresses at roughly 1cm/hr for a single baby and 2cm/hr for multiple births if the women's first pregnancy. Many midwifes become concerned at allocating times to these processes and think that they should be allowed to "take as long as it takes". This approach is fine but you need to have a continuous awareness of how tired the mother is, any evidence of fetal distress and signs they aren't progressing (not dilating). In second and subsequent pregnancies it is hugely variable, but is usually much faster.

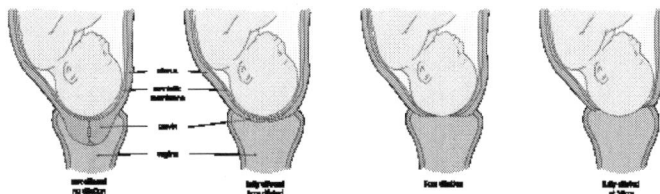

© Fred the Oyster

The first stage ends when the cervix is fully dilated about 10cm.

Care

Reassure patient. Allow then to assume whatever position they like.

Give entonox if you have it and the mum is distressed. Encourage patient to inhale at beginning of contraction to achieve maximum effect.

Problems in the first stage

Failure to progress is the biggest problem with the first stage and is discussed below together with failure to process in the second stage.

Second Stage of labour

The second stage of labour lasts from full dilation until the baby is delivered. Usually lasts between 1-2 hours, usually begins with an urge to push. It is worth checking internally when the women has a dire to push, that the cervix is fully dilated. Pushing against a cervix not fully dilated can cause it to become swollen and slow the process.

The usual position the baby is at the start of labour – occiput anterior (or OA). As the baby's head appears at the vulva. Its head rotates to face towards the mothers back. The back of the head delivers first followed by the face. The head then turns sideward to allow the shoulders to pass.

The shoulder nearest the front is delivered first followed by the other. The rest of the baby is then delivered.

Care

Support the head.

Once head delivered, check cord is not around neck. If so, slip over the head or double clamp and cut cord in between clamps.

Push gently on the head towards the rear will help deliver the first shoulder. Then push gently towards the mum's front to deliver the other shoulder.

Deliver the rest of the baby.

Dealing with the baby

Fortunately the baby will most of the time take care of itself provided you dry it and stimulate it; wrap it in a warm towel and put it to the breast.

If not crying or pinking up with 20-30 seconds, assess adequacy of ABC. Position the baby on its back – with its head in neutral position. Suction it nose and throat. If not breathing after this give 5 slow inflating breaths – either by using a resuscitation bag or your mouth – the volume of air is just a puff from within you cheeks. Feel for HR and if it is less than 60 start CPR. Continue to ventilate 20 times a minute and reassess at 5 minutes. If no response at this time in a austere environment, stop.

Placing the baby on the mothers breast stimulates the release of the hormone oxytocin with helps the uterus contract and to stop bleeding.

Problems in the second stage

Prolonged second stage

Usually once the cervix is fully dilated and the pushing starts the head (or presenting part) begins to descend through the pelvis and out of the birth canal. This process normally takes less than an hour, but 1-2 hrs at most. Slow descent often means the head is presenting abnormally. Instead of the occiput being at the front (OA), it may be at the rear (OP) or off to one side. This may also slow the first stage of labour and some women do not get to the second stage before requiring a caesarean section due to abnormal presentation.

The most important element here is time. With time the women will usually rotate the baby's head with contractions so it can be delivered.

If the baby gets stuck there two things will happen:

Mum will get exhausted

Baby will get distressed and die

The options are relatively limited here in the absence of being able to perform a caesarean section – which is discussed elsewhere. Forceps were developed for this reason but these are extremely dangerous in the hands of an untrained operator. If the baby is not delivered and the mum is becoming sick a destructive procedure on the baby may the only option – the head is what is stopping the delivery – decompressing the head, will usually allow delivery of the now dead baby.

An alternative if the head is low and does descend with contractions, but does not quite make it is an episiotomy.

Episiotomy

This is a surgical cut in the perineum (which essentially makes the hole the baby needs to come out bigger), the muscular area between the vagina and the anus. If the baby is distressed or stuck or if the baby's head is too large in relation to the opening and you think the tissue will tear very badly unless the opening from the vagina is carefully enlarged, then perform a Episiotomy. Either of two common cuts is made either in a straight line from the vulva towards the anus in a 6 o'clock position or preferably between the 7 and 8 o'clock position. Once the baby is delivered and stable, the incision can be closed with sutures.

Prolapsed cord

If the cord is visible through the vulva this is a life-threatening emergency for the baby, as the foetal circulation may be effected. Avoid handling the cord as it may cause it to spasm; place a large wet pad over it to keep it moist. If evacuation is not possible try to place it back inside. Carefully monitor mother and baby until evacuation is possible. Normally an emergency Caesarean section will need to be performed. The austere option is to allow the woman to labour and except the outcome.

Breech Presentations

If the babies bottom instead of the head presents this is known as a breech presentation. The problem is that the head is biggest part of the baby, and usually stretches the birth canal before delivery. If the bottom comes first then that dilation does not occur and there is risk of the head getting stuck.

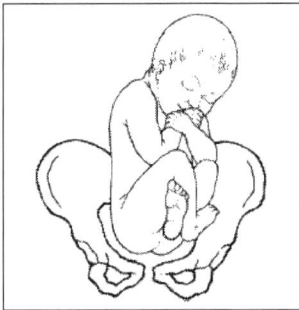

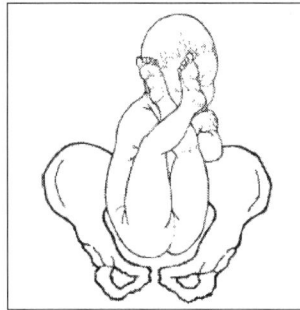

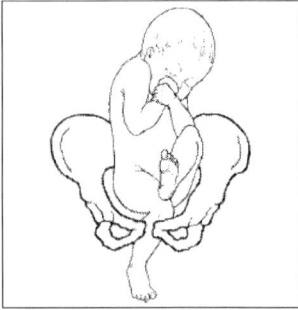

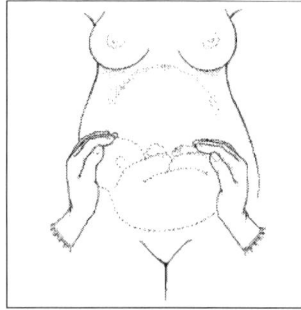

©WHO(2003)P.210

You may see baby's buttocks, genitalia, soles of feet or any limb. There are three types of breech:

Complete / Full – fully flexed foetus

Frank – extended legs

Footling / Incomplete – 1 or both thighs extended

A complete breech is the best sort and a footling breech the worst.

The diagnosis of breech can be tricky and even experienced midwives and obstetricians. Some signs of a breech include a longitudinal lie (not lying up or down, lying across), a hard head at fundus, the heart heard above the umbilicus. Ask mum where she feels the most kicks – up is good, down is bad. On a vaginal examination you do not feel the head in the pelvis and may feel a soft buttock or even an anus.

Delivery of the breech (Hands off is better!)

Gently allow the legs and body to be delivered, do not pull on then. The baby is usually looking backwards towards the mother bottom. Once the arms have been delivered allow the baby to hand with support for a minute or so before bringing the body up allowing the neck to extend and deliver the head. Frequently the head becomes stuck and this period of no oxygen can be sadly fatal to the baby.

Shoulder Dystocia

This is when the shoulder facing forward becomes stuck under the pelvic bone. There are a number of manoeuvres to aid in freeing it. A useful acronym for some of these is HELPER-R:

Help: Call for help if available.

Episiotomy: (Delay until other manoeuvre attempted) see below.

Legs: Flexing the mother's legs to her stomach. This widens the pelvis for 30-60 seconds (McRoberts Manoeuvre). If unsuccessful have someone else apply pressure to the lower abdomen (suprapubic pressure), and gently pull the baby's head.

Enter: Roll the mother over onto to her hands and knees, Position hands in vagina. Two fingers on front shoulder. Two fingers on back shoulder

Rotate anti-clockwise for 30-60 seconds (Rubin Manoeuvre)

Rotate clockwise for 30-60 seconds (Wood-Screw Manoeuvre)

Replace: If all manoeuvres fail, replace baby's head (Zavanelli Manoeuvre), as an emergency Caesarean section will need to be performed.

When performing any manoeuvre avoid the following:

Putting pressure on mothers abdomen

Excessive pulling on babies head or neck

Twisting or bending babies neck

Third Stage of Labour

Do not pull on the cord. The placenta 'after birth' will deliver within 20 minutes. Placenta delivery is stimulated by putting baby on mothers breast, which stimulates the release of oxytocin.

Problems with the third stage

Post-Partum Haemorrhage (PPH)

At the time of delivery the uterus has a blood flow of 250-300mls/min. Postpartum haemorrhage is defined as blood loss of greater than 500(+) mills, of blood, a major PPH is greater than 1000ml. If it occurs within 24 hours of the delivery it is known as a primary PPH, after 24 hours it is known as a secondary PPH.

Primary PPH:

There are four Main Causes:- a floppy uterus that is tired and wont contract, retained tissue, damage to the vagina or vulval region or a clotting problems

The risk factors for a primary PPH are a prolonged labour, a large uterus (big baby, twins, too much fluid), several previous labours, previous PPH, pre-eclampsia or a uterine abnormality.

Basic resuscitation:

2 x large bore IV lines – you need to be able to get fluid in faster than it comes out. IV fluid to maintain a blood pressure of >90mmHg. If possible pass a urethral catheter (a full bladder can contribute to poor contraction).

Gently rubbing the fundus (top) of the uterus through the abdomen will stimulate it to contract. It will contract poorly if still tissue in the uterus (see below).

Encourage the baby to feed which will help stimulate the uterus to contract.

Once more to record the level of the baby's response and to monitor its responsiveness the APGAR score is used.

Sign	0 Points	1 Point	2 Points
(A)ctivity	Absent	Arms and Legs Flexed	Active Movement
(P)ulse	Absent	< 100 bpm	> 100 bpm
(G)rimace	No Response	Grimace	Sneeze, cough, pulls away
(A)ppearance	Blue-gray, pale all over	Normal, except for extremities	Normal
(R)espiration	Absent	Slow, irregular	Good, crying

A score is taken at 1, 5 and 10 minute if required/

A score of:

7-10 is normal,

4-7 may require some resuscitation.

3 or below requires immediate resuscitation.

D13 Enhanced (Authorised Firearms Officers)

First Aid at Work; Initial and Requalification.
Target Group Authorised Firearms Officers.
Duration 4 days. Refresher training undertaken annually.

Learning Outcomes.
This module is the First Aider at Work (FAW) Standard as defined by the Health and Safety Executive (HSE).

This module will be further supplemented with the addition of the D13 enhanced tactical medicine that must be delivered by trainers who have experience in pre-hospital care.

It will involve moulages to replicate the provision of trauma care whilst in a conflict situation and the trainers will be assisted by a National Firearms Instructor.

Additional training will also be required for:

Use of nasopharyngeal airways.

Use of oropharyngeal airways.

Use of oxygen therapy.
Use of suction devices.
Use of haemostatic dressings.
Identification of wound management techniques including dressing and packing for all types of wounds.

Use of nasopharyngeal airways.

Nasopharyngeal Airways (NPAs) are semi-rigid plastic tubes that are inserted through the nose into the back of the throat.

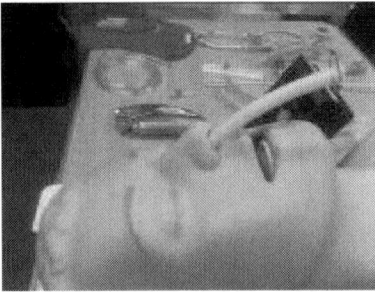

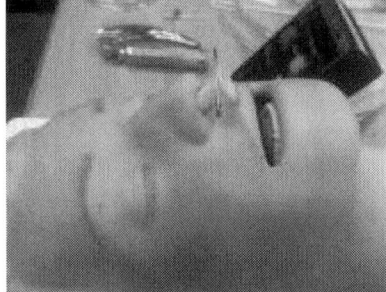

These should be used if there is damage to the jaw or swelling in the mouth which would make insertion of the oral airway difficult. They are either completely soft or with a solid distal end. When inserting the airway, check that the casualty's right nostril is not damaged; then if using the soft variety, place a safety pin through the end of the airway to prevent it being inhaled, insert using a twisting motion. If however the casualty has a fractured nose or you suspect they may have a fracture of the base of the skull, these should not be used as inserting them could cause additional damage. This method is not suitable for children under 6 years of age.

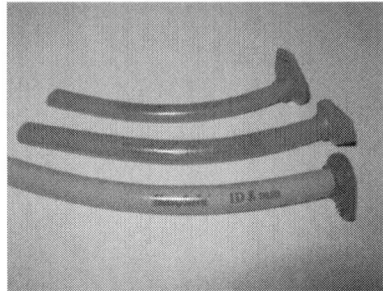

Use of Oropharyngeal Airway

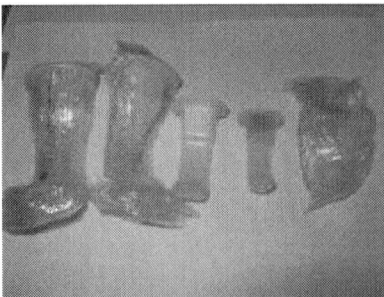

Oropharyngeal Airway OPAs are the easiest to insert and require little training or practice. They are slightly curved and flattened plastic tubes that when inserted lay on top of the tongue preventing it falling back and blocking the airway. They are available in a number of sizes and are suitable for infants, children and adults. To determine which size is suitable place one along the line of the jaw the correct size will be the distance between the corner of the mouth and the angle of the jaw.

Sizes and colours can vary with suppliers, common sizes in the UK are;

Colour	Size		Colour	Size
Yellow	5		White	1
Red	4		Black	0
Orange	3		Blue	00
Green	2		Clear	000

To insert an OPA, Use the following aide Memoire Invert, Insert, Rotate, Locate.

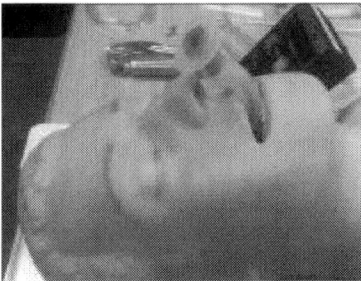

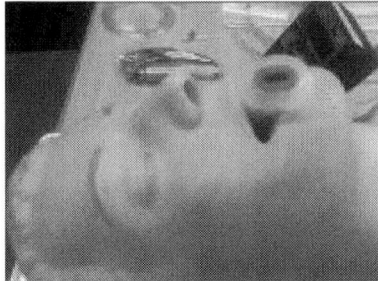

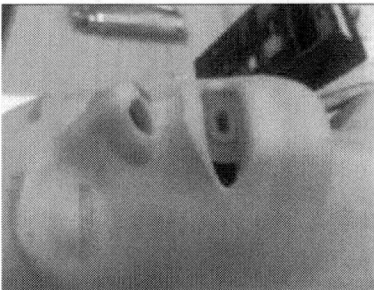

Locating OPA between teeth and lips will keep OPA in position.

Use of oxygen therapy.

Pulse Oximetry

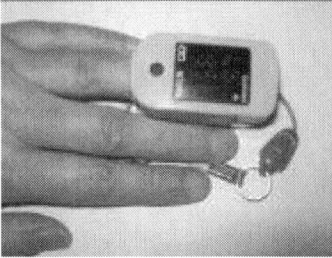

Pulse Oximetry is a way of monitoring the oxygenation of the patient's haemoglobin in their blood. A sensor is placed on a thin part of the patient's body, usually a fingertip, toe or earlobe. These devices are cheap and reliable and very useful.

Oxygen Therapy

Having the option of administering oxygen varies enormously in an austere situation. In someone who is profoundly hypoxic (low oxygen in their blood) there are limited options. However since the introduction of the British Thoracic Society Guidelines 2008 the amount of oxygen administered to patients has reduced considerably and many conditions we traditionally gave oxygen for (virtually everything) we no longer do, making the absence of oxygen for most patients less of a problem. Oxygen cylinders are generally black with a white collar (although they vary by country and are green in the USA). They have one or two connectors, the primary being a nipple and if there is a second it is often a Schrader valve, this allows connection to a ventilator or oxygen piping. On the top is a dial where the flow rate can be altered. Most allow between 1-15 L/min but others are more restrictive. The head also contains a gauge showing how much oxygen is remaining.

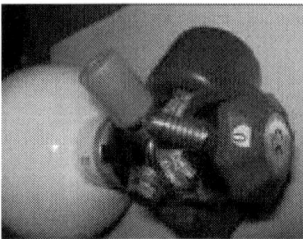

The key point to remember is that oxygen is given to provide adequate perfusion, not to cure breathlessness or push patients oxygen levels above what is normal for them as in the case of COPD.

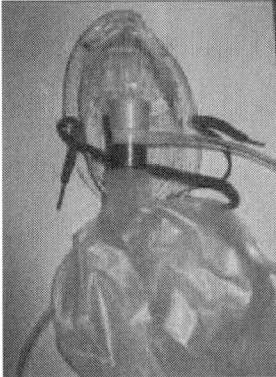

To give maximum concentration of oxygen through a non-rebreather mask first fill the attached bag with oxygen by keeping finger over inlet into mask until bag expands.

Some patients, who are classed as critically ill still need to receive High Flow oxygen i.e. 100% or 15/min through a non-rebreather mask. These include;

- Shock
- Sepsis
- Major Trauma
- Anaphylaxis
- Near Drowning
- Carbon Monoxide Poisoning
- Major Head Injury

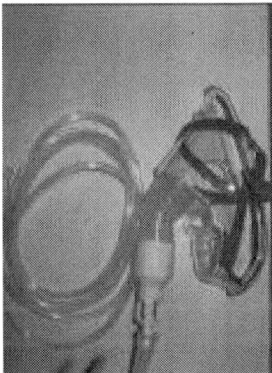

Other than in the above cases if the patient has COPD it likely their body is accustomed to surviving on lower concentration of oxygen. In this case oxygen is given if their oxygen saturation drops below 88%. Oxygen therapy is given via a 28% venture mask at 4L/Min to maintain a saturation of between 88% - 92%

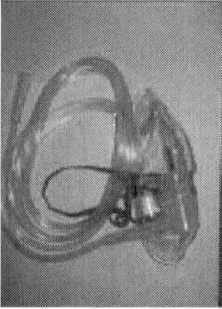

If the patient does not have a critical condition or COPD then give oxygen if saturation drops below 94%. Oxygen therapy is given via a simple mask at 8L/Min to maintain a saturation of 94%+. If you are unable to maintain saturations using this method, switch to a non-rebreather mask at 15L/min.

Using a Bag Valve Mask

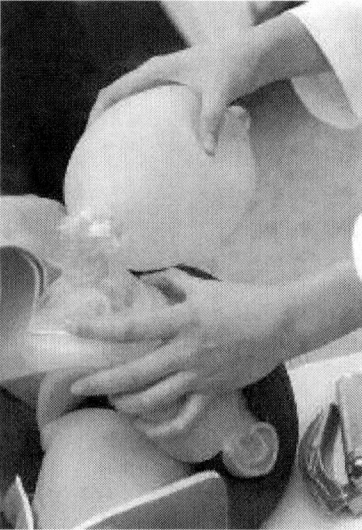

This device is for patients who are not breathing and require assistance. The Bag Valve Mask (BVM) is positioned over the casualty's mouth and nose. A seal is established by holding the mask with the first finger and thumb and curling the remaining fingers around their jaw. Where continuous ventilation is possible do so at a rate of 10-12 breathes per minute. To achieve the best seal the mask should be held in place with two hand and a second person should squeeze the bag.

© Mihail Syarov | Dreamstime.com

Use of Suction Devices.

If suction equipment is available to manage the airway use this to remove blood and debris from the mouth and throat, being careful not to trigger the gag reflex by inserting the suction catheter too far, which might cause fluid to move down to the lungs, a condition known as aspiration.

In order to prevent trauma to the mucous membranes inside the mouth manual suction should only be started once the catheter is within the mouth, automatic suction can be switched on but the hole in the catheter is only occluded once the catheter is inserted into the mouth as far as you can see.

If using automatic mains powered suction keep pressure for children between 80-100mmhg and for adults 80-120mmhg.

Slowly start to withdraw the catheter, rotating the catheter between finger and thumb as you do so and keeping it from touching the inside of the mouth. Always keep suction applied until the catheter is fully withdrawn from the mouth this will minimise leakage of secretions from the catheter.

Suction for a maximum of 10 seconds.

If the casualty has an oral or nasal airway in place which become blocked with secretions or vomit this can be suctioned with a small bore catheter. If this is time consuming the airway should be removed and replaced.

Monitor oxygen saturations and pause if dropping in a casualty that is breathing, in a casualty that is nor breathing clearing the airway takes priority.

Complications of suctioning can include;

- Oxygen de-saturation as indicated by pulse oximetry

- Damage to the mucous membranes

- Introducing Infection

- Causing irregular heart rhythms by stimulation the vagus nerve through keep suctioning

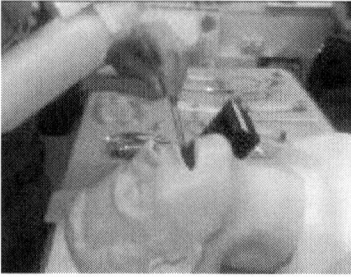

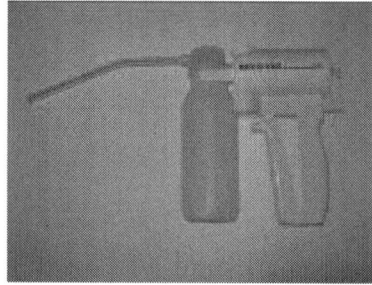

Use of haemostatic dressings.

Packing wounds

If a wound is deep it should be packed, avoid using anything fluffy like cotton wool. Instead, use plain gauze squares or ribbon gauze which is useful for small deep wounds as it can be fed in to the wound and packed down with forceps.

Tourniquet

The use of Tourniquets used to be discouraged but they have proved to be very effective in recent conflicts where severe bleeding from gunshot and explosions is prevalent.

A limb tourniquet can be improvised from any band of material 5-10cms wide. It should be applied 5-10cms above the wound and above the elbow or knee if the wound is on the lower part of the limb. Leave on for 30 minutes this will give you time to identify the point of injury and apply direct pressure. Ease off the tourniquet and if bleeding continues reapply. The application of a tourniquet rarely stops circulation completely but will slow it down enough for one of the other methods mentioned to be used effectively. The military have developed a Combat application tourniquet for just this purpose.

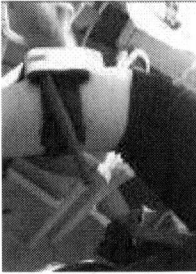

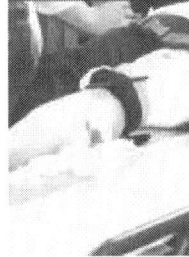

Haemostatic Agents

There are several different haemostatic agents such as Quikclot and Celox;

Quikclot

This was originally designed for the military although it has many civilian applications. It comes in its original form granules, Advanced Combat Sponges(ACS) and Combat Gauze. It works by absorbing the water content of blood and encouraging the bodies clotting system. The reaction causes heat to be generated which originally caused some problems this has now been rectified. QuikClot must be applied to the blood vessel itself. Contamination, dirt or accumulated blood has to be removed for it to be effective.

Celox

This is a similar product, made entirely from natural materials making it more easily absorbable in the body. It is available as granules, as gauze and in an applicator for deep penetrating wounds.

Hemcon

Made from chitosan the Hemcon dressing sticks to a wound and promotes clotting whilst providing an anti-microbial barrier. Available in a variety of sizes. It is expensive compared to other similar products.

Gunshot Wounds, Explosions & Tactical Considerations

Gunshot Wounds

Introduction

Gunshot wounds can be split into two groups depending on the muzzle velocity of the weapon. Generally handguns are considered as low velocity weapons with a muzzle velocity below 1000 ft/sec and can be fired with one hand, whereas a rifle is high velocity weapon with a velocity of greater than 1000 ft/sec.

Exceptions to this are high calibre handguns such as .357 and .44 Magnum, which are usually fired with two hands and are treated as high-velocity and .22 Rifles and Shotguns at long range that are considered low-velocity weapons.

The difference is mainly academic as the extent of wounds caused by firearms is determined by many factors including the deformation and fragmentation of the projectile, its entrance profile and the path travelled through the body.

Most handgun wounds can be treated without surgery and with careful wound care management; although fractures are likely if the projectile hits bone. Even if the wound appears clean contamination is common and prophylactic antibiotic therapy is recommended. If open fractures are present intravenous antibiotic therapy for 48 to 72 hours is preferred or a full course of oral antibiotics.

Rifles and shotguns at close range cause high velocity wounds. Due to the characteristics of high velocity rounds the chance of open fractures and wound contamination is much higher than with handguns. In high velocity injury tissues are pushed away around the projectile path this is known as temporary a cavity. The effect produces blunt trauma that extends beyond the tissue actually contacted by the projectile if the tissue retains its contractility this cavity will disappear when the tissue returns to its normal position. The pulsation of the cavity results in a strong negative pressure that draws contamination from both the entry and exit wounds along the entire wound tract.

However even with high velocity wounds if there is only a small amount of tissue damage, no fragmentation or fractures then simple wound care may be enough.

Ballistics

In addition to the range and calibre of the weapon we must also consider the type of ammunition that is used. A normal military bullet is coated with a solid metal jacket and is less likely to fragment when it passes through the body, additional fragments may occur when a jacketed bullet fragments when hitting bone or when a non-jacketed, soft-point, hollow-point, or composite bullet fragments when passing through soft tissue thus creating larger permanent cavities by mushrooming out. Fragmentation may significantly increase injury. Should the cavity at the point become plugged with clothing, wood or other debris it may fail to expand.

Some Military rounds are designed to tumble in flight and thus create a larger tract and more damage. Civilian rounds such as the Black Talon, Hydra-Shok, or Golden Saber are designed to ensure complete transference of the kinetic energy to the target. Whilst other rounds may achieve over penetration and pass through the body without fragmenting, thus not impart all of its energy.

A shotgun blast creates multiple projectiles creating numerous holes and significant tissue damage, especially at close range. A variant bullet is the composite round. These have a copper hollow point outer shell containing shot stabilised with epoxy resin which fragment upon hitting a surface, creating multiple projectiles once they enter the body. This dramatically increases the size of the permanent cavity.

Even blank ammunition containing powder but no bullet may cause injury or death at close range due to the gases, heat and packing released when fired.

Care Under Fire

If a member of you team is hit and active fire is still present;

Return fire if appropriate and take cover.

Encourage casualty to take cover and avoid taking additional wounds

Any casualties should be extricated from burning vehicles or buildings and moved to places of relative safety. Do what is necessary to stop the burning process.

Stop catastrophic haemorrhage using combat dressings and tourniquet.

Disarm casualties with an altered mental status.

Evaluating the Casualty

Both knowledge and practice is needed to properly assess a firearms injury, when evaluating a wound interview any witnesses to determine both the range and angle the bullet entered from and the type of weapon used. Ask how many shots were heard, as the bullets will need to be accounted for. Any bullets or fragments removed or found should be retained to try and ascertain if all parts of the round were recovered and nothing is left within the wound.

If there are any spent cartridges cases or shell casings around these can be examined to determine both the weapon used and its calibre

Carry out a full secondary survey and instigate any life saving measures as you progress. Whilst examining the body check for additional injuries as well as entry and exit wounds. Assume that there may be both fractures and neurological damage until proven otherwise.

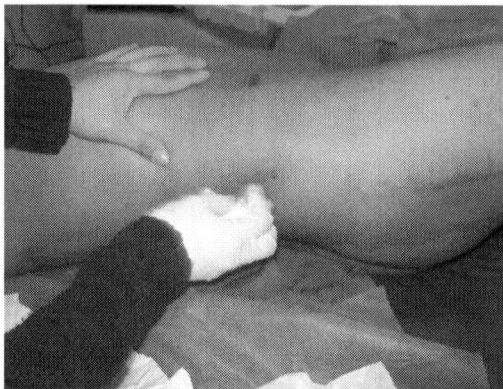

©Bobjgaalindo

Types of Wounds from firearms.

The primarily mechanism of injury is the path the projectile takes when it passes through the body. A shotgun loaded with shot as opposed to a solid load fired at close will produce a large entrance wound, but will usually lack the energy to penetrate the body completely. The entry wound from a rifle or handgun may be more difficult to locate as the small diameter of a projectile and elastic property of the skin will close the wound once the bullet has passed through.

A shot fired at point blank range may exhibit charring to the clothing or skin from the muzzle flash and hot gasses escaping from the barrel when fired. A stellate, or star-shaped, wound is formed at the skin with a jagged appearance to the entrance wound and sometimes, an imprint of the barrel is left in the skin. Complications can occur from this as the gasses are transmitted into the wound making the temporary cavity larger and carrying soot and charred clothing into the cavity to further contaminate the wound.

Conversely exit wounds tend to be larger and will contain whatever debris the bullet has sucked through the body. Also even if only one shot is fired the bullet may have fragmented within the body and created more than one exit wound or propelled bony fragments through the skin.

The second injuring mechanism is the temporary cavity created by the kinetic energy of the projectile This can cause tissue to be forced from the projectiles path, causing stretching, tearing and concussive forces to the surrounding tissue. The cavity may measure 15 times the projectile diameter. During the first five minutes, the wall collapses and reforms (pulsates) several times. This additional sheering force can damage tissue some distance from the projectile tract itself.

Wounds to the chest or abdomen will frequently incur Organ damage, observe for signs of air *(pneumothorax)* or blood *(haemothorax)* in the space between the chest wall and the lungs, which may cause one lung to collapse or compression of the heart (Cardiac Tamponade) by the presence of blood or fluid in the sac surrounding the heart *(Pericardium)* or damage to the organs in the abdomen. Not forgetting to check under the armpit and in the space between the genitals and the anus *(perineum)* for entrance and exit wounds.

Treatment

Airway Management

Chin lift or jaw thrust manoeuvre

Nasopharyngeal airway

Place in the recovery position.

Consider Advanced Airway Procedures

Breathing

Consider the possibility of a tension Pneumothorax in any casualty with progressive respiratory distress with trauma of the torso. (See chest decompression)

Apply an occlusive dressing to any open chest wound and monitor for signs of a tension Pneumothorax.

Nightingale Occlusive Dressing

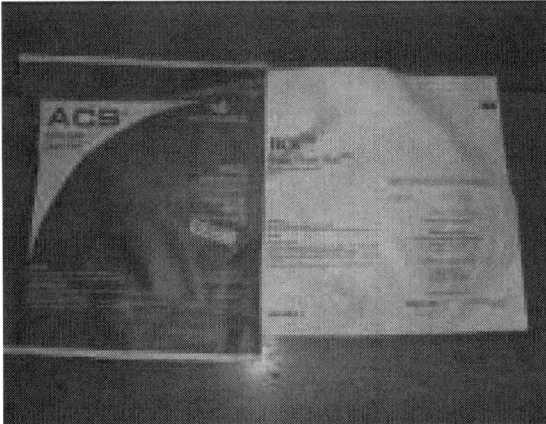

If available use an Asherman chest seal or Bolin chest seal to cover the wound this will allow air out of the chest but prevent more from being sucked in. If there is more than one wound place occlusive dressings over the others.

Bleeding

Check under hollows of body for unrecognised haemorrhage and control any bleeding, using tourniquet, combat dressings or haemostatic agents (Combat Gauze, Quikclot Granules or Celox) with 3 minutes of direct pressure. Apply any tourniquets 5-10cm above wound. For high leg wounds where tourniquet is not appropriate a device such as a Combat Ready Clamp (CRoC) can be used.

See below for Ballistic injury pack including;

Blast Bandage

Olaes Dressing

Nightingale Dressing

Celox Gauze

Combat Application Tourniquet

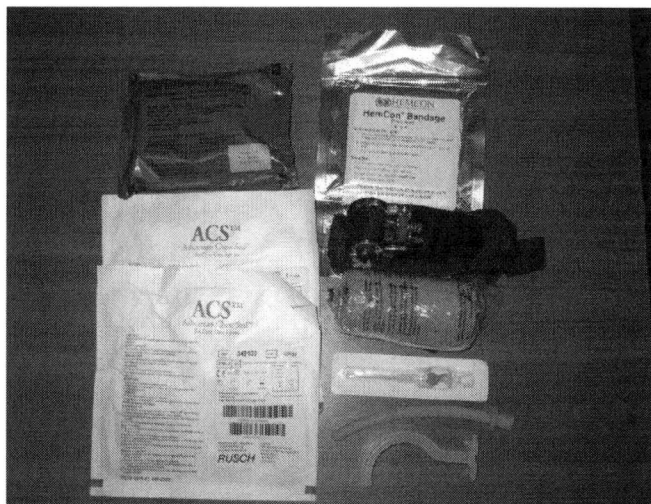

Blowout bag: Personal medical equipment for a tactical situation (Dressings, HemCon bandages, Asherman Chest seals, oral and nasal airways, iv cannular and a tourniquet).

If a distal pulse is still present and bleeding still active, tighten tourniquet or apply a second one to stem bleeding.

Ensure all tourniquet sites are exposed and time of application is recorded on white tab of tourniquet using an indelible marker.

Prevention of hypothermia

Minimise casualty's exposure to the elements. Keep clothing on or replace wet clothing if available. Place casualty on insulated surface as soon as possible. Cover with space blanket, blizzard survival blanket, Ready-Heat Blanket or similar devices to keep casualty warm and dry.

Penetrating Eye Trauma

If a penetrating eye injury is noted or suspected:

a) Perform a rapid field test of visual acuity.

b) Cover the eye with a rigid eye shield (NOT a pressure patch.)

c) Ensure that the 400 mg moxifloxacin tablet in the combat pill pack is taken if possible and that IV/IM antibiotics are given as outlined below if oral moxifloxacin cannot be taken.

Monitoring

Record patients pulse, respiration rate and if available oxygen saturations using pulse oximetry

Wounds & Fractures

Perform more thorough check for wounds and check known wounds are correctly dressed. Any fractures should be splinted and distal limbs checked for Movement, Sensation and Circulation(MSC) before and after splinting to ensure neurovascular system has not been compromised by injury or immobilisation.

Burns

Burns of the face, particularly with soot around mouth and nose can indicate smoke inhalation. These casualties need their respiration rates and oxygen saturations carefully monitored and may need intubation or a surgical airways.

Estimate percentage burnt using the Rule of nines (see burns section).Cover burns with dry, sterile dressings, or gel bun dressings and cling film if available. If burns are >20% protect as for hypothermia above and start slow IV fluids max 1000ml. If hemorrhagic shock is also present this should be treated as above.

Cardiopulmonary resuscitation

Casualties with blast or penetrating trauma who have no pulse, no ventilations, and no other signs of life, should not be resuscitated. However those with chest trauma should have bilateral needle decompression performed before stopping care to ensure they don't have a tension Pneumothorax.

Documentation & Communication

Document injuries received, treatment given and observations recorded with relevant times. At all times explain care and reassure casualty

(Adapted from the Tactical Combat Casualty Care Guidelines)

Post Tactical Casualty Care

With all gunshot wounds the area must be thoroughly explored to remove fragments and any remaining projectiles. The wound needs to be irrigated and cleaned, if dead tissue (4 Cs colour, consistency, contractility, and capacity to bleed) is present in or adjacent to the wound this needs to be removed. Dead tissue is removed (debridement) until surrounding healthy tissue is exposed in order to promote healing and knitting of the wound edges. If there is damage to blood vessels, exploration and repair should be performed after fractures are stabilised.

In circumstances in which contaminated dead (*necrotic*) tissue cannot be excised promptly or adequately, a prophylactic antibiotic cream, beads, solution or spray should be applied directly to the wound to prevent otherwise lethal infection.

When assessing possible nerve damage, lack of feeling or control in extremities is not always an indication for extensive exploration for as the loss may be temporary and feeling return without further intervention.

If substantial open fractures occur it will not be possible to stabilise them in the field as surgical plates, nailing or external fixation will be required. These types of injuries require the services of an orthopaedic surgeon.

The injuries considered above are mainly associated with wounds to the limbs or flesh wounds to the trunk. Deep penetrating wounds to the chest or abdomen will effect single or multiple organs, all these injuries are potentially life threatening as the loss of function of the organ, internal bleeding and high risk of infection have far reaching effects.

It is possible to survive some organ damage without restorative surgery such as a collapsed lung or damage to one kidney providing good care is given, bleeding is controlled and infection prevented. However most organ injuries would be fatal without professional care.

In all cases the following steps need to be taken (see Relevant Chapters)

Bleeding must be controlled.

Fractures Stabilised

Dead tissue removed from wounds (*debridement*)

The wound or wounds cleaned and washed out (*irrigated*).

If necessary the wound/s should be packed or closed as appropriate.

Explosions

An explosion is the violent expansion of a substance caused by the gases released during rapid combustion. One effect of an explosion is a shock wave, this cause extreme compression of molecules in surrounding air or water creating an over pressure. This wave travels outward from the centre and as it does so part of the force is dissipated into any objects in its path. Most casualties within the injury radius of an explosion will commonly have penetrating, blunt, and burn. When the blast wave contacts the human body, the shock wave causes stress-induced tears in any open air filled spaces, which result in internal bleeding and weakening of the tissue. Secondary problems can occur due to rupture as air escapes from along the respiratory tract or spillage of gastrointestinal (GI) contents.

Primary injuries

Primary injuries are caused by initial explosion and shock waves, ear drums can burst, brain haemorrhages can occur, damage to lungs and other hollow organs such as the intestines, not all injuries may be immediately apparent. Injuries can result in shock and respiratory failure.

As the blast wave will damage structures injuries are commonly caused through structural collapse as much as primary blast damage. Individuals in buildings or vehicles are at greater risk as are those in body armour, but their risk of secondary blast injury from fragments, shrapnel, and debris due to its ballistic protection of vital structures is decreased. Think beyond obvious injuries and consider the mechanism to determine possible underlying injuries.

Amputations

In high explosive detonations traumatic amputations can be caused by blast wave.

Potential injuries to lungs;

Hemorrhage:

Pulmonary contusion

Hemoptysis

Hemothorax

Escape of Air:

Pneumothorax

Pulmonary pseudocyst

Arterial gas embolism (AGE)

For detailed assessment technique see the relevant chapter, increasing symptoms that develop over time can indicate a worsening condition. Determine if they are short of breath?, do they have normal breath and percussion sounds? Any chest pain?

Primary Blast Lung Injury (BLI)

Caused by ruptures of alveolar and peri-vascular hemorrhages. Casualties with BLI will show signs of acute respiratory failure within minutes of an explosion. Casualties with penetrating head or torso injuries, multiple injuries or bums >10% of surface area are at high risk of BLI.

Potential injuries to GI Tract;

Symptoms from GI injuries may not shown until upto 48 hours after injury.

- Hemorrhage:
- Hematoma leading to obstruction
- Upper or lower GI bleeding
- Hemoperitoneum
- Escape of Contents:
- Mediastinitis
- Peritonitis

Do they have any abdominal or genital pain, nausea, vomiting, urge to pass, or blood in urine or stools, diarrhoea, haematemesis.?

Any unexplained hypotension or fever?

Potential problems to Head, Eyes, Ears, Nose or Throat (HEENT);

Head & Base of Skull fracture

Check for Blood or CSF from Ears, Nose or Mouth

Racoon Eyes (Bruising around Eyes) or Battle sign (bruising behind ear)

Initial Blast waves can cause loss of memory, confusion, headache and disorientation. Long term damage can cause traumatic Brain Injury (TBI) and Post Traumatic Stress Disorder (PTSD)

Eye Injury

Do they have eye pain or vision problems?

Any trauma to face or eye lid?

Middle ear:

Ruptured tympanic membrane (TM)

Temporary conductive hearing loss

Inner ear:

Permanent or temporary sensory hearing loss

Tinnitus

Do they have ear pain or hearing problems?

Any foreign material in the ear?

Facial or Sinus Injuries

Maxillary or mandibular fractures

Blowout fractures of orbit (Underlying

Teeth fractures

Secondary injuries

Secondary injuries are caused by casualties being hit by debris, which is thrown by the explosion, some can cause blunt trauma whilst others will cause penetrating injuries including impalements. In explosions caused by ignition of fuel; burns are highly likely.

Tertiary injuries

Tertiary injuries are caused by impact injuries from the casualty being thrown in the air and landing on or against a hard surface. Fractures and head injuries are common tertiary injuries as well as contusions and laceration too solid organs such as the spleen, liver and kidney.

Quaternary injuries

Are miscellaneous effects such as burns, contamination and infection caused by debris, chemical release, and smoke inhalation or CBRN elements. Underlying medical conditions such as asthma may be worsened by inhalation of smoke. If caught in a structure that collapses there is also a danger of crush injuries.

Underwater Explosions

A shock wave moves more quickly and is more pronounced in water than in air because of the relative incompressibility of liquids. Because the human body is mostly water and incompressible, an underwater shock wave passes through the body with little or no damage to the solid tissues. However, the air spaces of the body, even though they may be in pressure balance with the ambient pressure, do not readily transmit the overpressure of the shock wave. As a result, the tissues that line the air spaces are subject to a violent fragmenting force at the interface between the tissues and the gas. The amount of damage to the body is influenced by a number of factors. These include the size of the explosion, the distance from the site, and the type of explosive. The depth of water and the type of bottom, which can reflect and amplify the shock wave) may also have an effect, under average conditions, a shock wave of 500 psi or greater will cause injury to the lungs and intestinal tract. The extent of injury is also determined in part by the degree to which the diver's body is submerged. For an underwater blast, any part of the body that is out of the water is not affected.

Conversely, for an air blast, greater depth provides more protection. The maximum shock pressure to which a diver should be exposed is 50 psi. The safest and recommended procedure is to have all divers leave the water if an underwater explosion is planned or anticipated. A diver who anticipates a nearby underwater explosion should try to get all or as much of his body as possible out of the water. If in the water, the diver's best course of action is to float face up, presenting the thicker tissues of the back to the explosion. Personnel treading water are at higher risk for abdominal than thoracic blast injury from underwater explosion whereas Fully submerged personnel are at equal risk of combined thoracic and abdominal blast injury, as are personnel in open air, but equivalency occurs at three times distance from explosion underwater compared to open air.   (US Navy Dive Manual FM 20-1)

Tactics and Medicine

Most of the material in this book can be used in a tactical situation. However military medicine does have some unique factors which are described below.

Whereas in the past explosive trauma generally killed its victim outright the use of modern body armour now provides better protection to the head, chest and abdomen, making wounds more survivable. The upshot of this is that extremity wounds are often severe but survivable.

Initial care in an operational situation is provided if possible by the individual themselves or other members of the team as all will have basic first aid skills, which is called 'Care under fire" in the military, secondary care is by the team medics who have additional training. The next level is by Combat Medical Technicians (CMTs) or Civilian EMTs and paramedics. The final in theatre care given by Nurses and Doctors based at a Hospital. Current military procedures aims to get the casualty to a hospital within two hours from time of injury in the meantime the casualty needs to be stabilised and treated, this compares with a preferred on scene time of less than 10 minutes and a surgical option being available within an hour of injury in a civilian setting.

The civilian ABC approach has been replaced with <C>ABC where the first priority is given to stopping catastrophic haemorrhage. In these circumstances there is little point in securing a person's airway or supporting breathing if they are going to bleed out whilst you are doing it.

Military medics use haemostatic agents, chest seals, field dressings and tourniquets to control bleeding. Their use is discussed in detail in the trauma section under wound management.

Use of simple adjuncts such as airways oral and nasal airways are used in both settings, but in a tactical situation surgical cricothyroidotomy are used in preference to intubation. This is partly due to the technique and the use of a lighted laryngoscope in a potentially hostile situation.

In civilian trauma the mechanism is usually by blunt force which has a higher probability of damage to the neck (C-spine), in military situation where the mechanism is usually through penetrating trauma the likelihood is much less. Therefore the normal procedure of immobilising a casualty is left to the hospital staff to decide this enables the casualty to be moved faster and more easily away from the point of injury. The use of a spinal collar alone does not provide complete immobilisation but may be considered as an aid, if a purpose made collar is unavailable it can be fashioned from a Sam splint.

For the delivery of drugs and fluids the intraosseous (IO) route is preferred to IV access as the circulatory systems of military casualty is often impaired due to shock and multiple limb injuries.

Personal Protective and Riot Control Weapons

Taser

The first shock weapon was developed in 1969, there have been many models and improvements. Pistols are now available which fire three rounds without the need to reload and recently a shotgun type weapon has been deployed by some police forces.

The Taser fires two small dart-like electrodes which are pointed to penetrate clothing and barbed to prevent removal, they stay connected to the gun unit by wires and are propelled by small compressed gas charge, ranges vary between 4-10 meters. The Taser uses a electric current to disrupt voluntary control of muscles. Someone hit by a Taser experiences an overloading of stimulation to their motor and sensory nerves, resulting in strong involuntary muscle contractions. Once the electricity stops flowing the subject immediately regains control of his body.

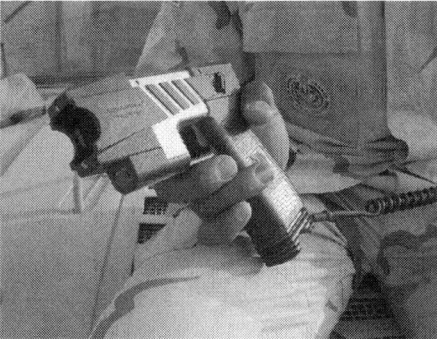
©US Army

Some Taser models, have a "Drive Stun" capability, where the Taser is held against the target without firing the projectiles, and is intended to cause pain without incapacitating the target. Although used widely by military and police forces around the world in some countries they are banned and considered a torture device.

©jasonesbain

Although much safer than other stopping techniques there have been some deaths associated with the use of Tasers as they can potentially generate an irregular heart beat (cardiac arrhythmias) which can lead to a heart attack or Cardiac Arrest. It has also been suggested that targets with serious mental health issues or under the influence of narcotics have suffered additional harm as the result of being tasered, however this is still controversial.

From a medical stand point the barbs can be removed and the needles withdrawn from the skin. If cardiac monitoring or ECGs are available it should be done to rule out the presence of an irregular heart beat.

Pepper Spray

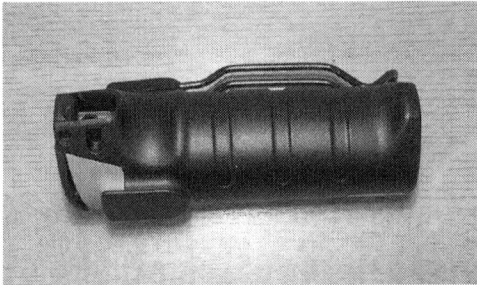
©Mattes

Pepper spray contains an extract of chili (capsicum), it irritates the tear ducts causing excess tear production, pain, temporary blindness which lasts from 15–30 minutes, a burning sensation of the skin which lasts from 45 to 60 minutes, upper body spasms which force a person to bend forward and uncontrollable coughing making it difficult to breathe or speak for between 3 to 15 minutes. Pepper spray causes swelling (inflamation). It causes immediate closing of the eyes, difficulty breathing, runny nose, and coughing. The duration depends on the strength but the average full effect lasts 30 to 45 minutes, with lesser effects lasting for hours. A single dose is relatively harmless to the eyes but repeated doses make the eye more sensitive to irritation.

There are also synthetic variants available. Most effects are temporary although in rare cases deaths have occurred following deployment against persons with asthma or who were subject to restraining techniques which restricted their breathing.

 It is either delivered via an aerosol or sometimes as a ball similar to a paint ball these projectiles also contain dyes, either visible or UV-reactive, to mark an attacker's skin and/or clothing to enhance identification by police.

Pepper spray is not soluble in water, trials have suggested that there is no one definitive treatment for removing it although many ambulance services in the USA carry baby shampoo for this purpose. Casualties should be encouraged to blink repeatedly, which will help flush the irritant from the eyes. Do not let them rub affected parts as this will spread the contamination.

Mace

Mace is a branded irritant spray often with the same contents as pepper spray but sometimes using a synthetic chemical compound and occasionally partly tear gas. Treatment is the same as above.

Tear Gas (CS Gas)

©Ντουντούκα

Tear gas is a synthetic chemical weapon used in riot control, it is often deployed via spray, gas grenades or canisters fired from projectiles. Individuals deploying this will need to wear respirators to protect themselves. It is actually a white acidic powder with a peppery smell not a gas.

Tear gas stimulates the corneal nerves in the eyes and irritating mucous membranes in the eyes, nose, mouth and lungs, this causes severe burning sensation, crying, sneezing, coughing, difficulty breathing, panic, nausea and vomiting, pain in the eyes and temporary blindness. The blood pressure rises, and the breathing and heart rate slow. It also causes a burning sensation on any skin exposed to it

Antidote

Because tear gas is not actually a gas but a very fine acid powder, its effectiveness can be easily mitigated by any over the counter anti acid such as Campden tablets, Sodium bicarbonate or Alka-Seltzer.

Exposure

If you are accidently exposed to CS gas, hold your breath and almost completely close your eyes. If you can get to an area of fresh air the effects wear off in a few minutes if not cover your face with a clean cloth, as it is a powder not a gas this should minimize inhalation. Keep your mouth closed as breathing it in through your mouth will cause coughing and possibly vomiting.

Clothes will remain coated with dust particles so once clean brush them down and wash clothes separately from others to remove particles.

Appendix 1 Medical Terminology

Although You may never hopefully need to know what all those long medical words mean. It is useful to have an understanding of the basics. It means you can converse with medics and if you intend to read more on medical subjects you will know some of the terminology already.

Like most words medical terminology are split into two or more parts, common suffix and prefix's are given below.

a-	Absence of
-ab	Away From
-ad	Towards
Ante-	In Front off
Arthro-	Joint
Brady-	Slow
Cardio-	Heart
Cholecyst	Gall Bladder
Crani-	Skull
Dys-	dysfunction, disorder, difficult or painful
Gastr(o)	Stomach
Glycol-	sugar
Heme-	Blood
Hemato-	Blood
Hemi-	Half
Hepat-	Liver
Hyper-	High, Above, Excess
Hypo-	Low
My(o)-	Muscle
Nephr(o)	Kidney
Neuro-	Nerve
Onco-	Tumour
Osseo	Bony
Oste(o)	Bone
Pneumo-	Lung
Thorac-	Rib Cage

-algia	Pain
-ectomy	Removed by surgery
-emia	to do with blood
-itis	inflammation
-oma	Tumour or swelling
-pathy	Disease
-pepsia	Digestion
-plegia	paralysis
-pnoea	breathing
-tension	Pressure
-uria	Urine

i.e. A-pnoea	is no breathing
Dys-pnoea)	is difficulty breathing
Tachy- pnoea	is fast breathing
Hypo-glyca-emia	is Low sugar in Blood

Printed in Great Britain
by Amazon